A PREFACE TO

AUSTEN

CHRISTOPHER GILLIE

REVISED EDITION

D0144877

Longman

An imprint of **Pearson Education**

Harlow, England · London · New York · Reading, Massachusetts · San Francisco
Toronto · Don Mills, Ontario · Sydney · Tokyo · Singapore · Hong Kong · Seoul
Taipei · Cape Town · Madrid · Mexico City · Amsterdam · Munich · Paris · Milan

To my daughter, Jane

Christopher Gillie is an Arts Tutor for the Open University having for a long period served Trinity Hall, Cambridge as a lecturer in English. Among other books he has compiled the *Longman Companion to English Literature* and in 1983 published the volume on E M Forster for the present series.

Pearson Education Limited
Edinburgh Gate
Harlow
Essex CM20 2JE
England

and Associated Companies throughout the world

Visit us on the World Wide Web at:
www.pearsoneduc.com

First published 1974
Revised edition 1985

ISBN 0 582 43762 8 PPR

British Library Cataloguing-in-Publication Data
A catalogue record for this book can be obtained from the
British Library

Library of Congress Cataloging-in-Publication Data
A catalog record for this book can be obtained from the
Library of Congress

10 9 8 7 6 5 4 3 2 1
04 03 02 01

Set in 10/11pt Baskerville MT

Produced by Pearson Education Asia (Pte) Ltd.,
Printed in Singapore (KKP)

PREFACE BOOKS

General Editor: JOHN PURKIS

'A description of what the *Preface Books* were intended to be was included in the first volume and has appeared unchanged at the front of every succeeding title: "A series of scholary and critical studies of major writers intended for those needing modern and authoritative guidance through the characteristic difficulties of their work to reach an intelligent understanding and enjoyment of it." This may seem modest enough but a moment's reflection will reveal what a considerable claim it actually is. It is much to the credit of Longman and to their (founding) editor Maurice Hussey and his authors that these words have come to seem no more than a plain statement of fact.'

NATE NEWS

Chawton. The cottage belonged to Jane Austen's brother Edward. He gave it to the widowed Mrs Austen in 1809. The first four of Jane Austen's novels were published while she lived here, and she only left in 1817 when she moved to Winchester where in a few months she died.

Contents

PART THREE: THE ART OF JANE AUSTEN

PART FOUR: REFERENCE SECTION

List of Illustrations

Acknowledgements

I would like to record my gratitude to the General Editor, Maurice Hussey, for much useful advice, and particularly for drawing my attention to material for illustrations, to Professor Nikolaus Pevsner's essay, 'The Architectural Setting of Jane Austen's Novels' (*Journal of the Warburg and Courtauld Institute*, Vol. 31, 1968) which is the source of our maps of Bath and London and to D. J. Greene's essay, 'Jane Austen and the Peerage' (*Publications of the Modern Language Association of America*, Vol. 68, 1953).

The author and publisher are grateful to the following for permission to reproduce photographs:

Jane Austen Society and J. Butler Kearney, pages 33 and 148; Bath Municipal Libraries and Victoria Art Gallery, pages 25 and 111; Bristol City Art Gallery, page 84; British Museum, pages 19 and 127; British Tourist Authority, *frontispiece*; J. Butler Kearney, page 160; Courtauld Institute, page 117; Glasgow Art Gallery and Museum, page 130; A.F. Kersting, page 134; Major E. Knight and J. Butler Kearney, page 6 *below*; Mansell Collection, page 11; National Portrait Gallery, pages 29, 44 *both*, 52 *both*, 69 and 81; BBC Hulton Picture Library, pages 78 and 114; University Library Cambridge, pages 92 *both* and 179.

The painting of Bath by J. C. Nattes is reproduced on the cover by permission of the British Library.

Foreword

The centre of the world of Jane Austen lay in and near the county of Hampshire and had its outposts, usually for comparative purposes, in London, Lyme Regis, Bath and one or two areas not exactly on the map. All these locations are dominated by families, often obsessed with finance and the prospects of matrimonial alliances and occasionally alarmed by the unsatisfactory status of newcomers to the district. To accompany these observations she undoubtedly had notions of the appropriate architectural contexts though, as Sir Nikolaus Pevsner pointed out, she spent rather too little time in visualizing and verbalizing them. In this book we have provided one or two of such settings, but Christopher Gillie's main purpose has been to explore the social and moral themes that emerge from the conversations that provide the matrix of the novels. If they are social comedies they are shown to be also dramas of the conscience, the mind and the imagination that derive from the eighteenth-century situations and idioms which she recreated.

For the Revised Edition of this most successful study Mr Gillie has turned to several new and revealing topics and reviewed some of the most distinguished criticism and scholarship of the last decade. Social and political attitudes associated with the opening of the nineteenth century are prominently discussed on pages 59–61 and 99–101. A chronological table has been provided to help the reader define for himself the context of the popular and seminal novels associated always with her name. How we should read them today in order to understand the universal truths that nourish them is the preoccupation of the modern commentator, and to set these out in the most cogent manner has been Christopher Gillie's special concern in these pages.

MAURICE HUSSEY
General Editor

Maurice Hussey died suddenly in June 1991. The Publishers and author would like to pay tribute to his wisdom, inspiration and friendship as Editor of Preface Books. He will be sadly missed.

Introduction

'What do you read, Mr Masson?' said Mrs Merry.

'Very little off my own line, Mrs Merry. Miss Austen is the novelist I read the most.'

'What do you think of her books, Mr Fletcher?' said Delia to Francis.

'I am afraid, Miss Bentley, that I have very little use for books written by ladies for ladies, if I may so express myself; though I dare say I should be the better for them.'

'Oh, no, you would not. You could not be,' said Bumpus.

'It is the other way round,' said Masson.

IVY COMPTON-BURNETT: *Pastors and Masters* (1925)

Ivy Compton-Burnett, from whose second novel this extract is taken, invariably set her stories at the end of the nineteenth century or the beginning of this one. The conversation suggests fairly enough Jane Austen's reputation at the time: she was admired by a literary elite, including Tennyson, Macaulay, George Lewes and George Eliot; she was despised by the solemn, the pompous, the obtuse and the humourless. But she was also enjoyed by very many who found in her an assured and reassuring world for escape from the restless questionings of their own.

In the twentieth century a change has come about; the novelist Ivy Compton-Burnett to some extent illustrates it. No other novelist of distinction carried the mark of Jane Austen's influence so clearly, and yet her novels are sharp, pitiless, pessimistic analyses of human relations. The change is further indicated by this sentence from an essay entitled 'Regulated hatred: an aspect of the work of Jane Austen,' by D. W. Harding, first published in 1940 in *Scrutiny*: 'Her books are, as she meant them to be, read and enjoyed by precisely the sort of people whom she disliked: she is a literary classic of the society which attitudes like hers, held widely enough, would undermine.' How has this change come about—the change which has replaced Jane Austen the tranquillizer for the overstressed by Jane Austen the 'truth-teller' as Laurence Lerner has designated her?

Although she had discriminating admirers in the nineteenth century, none of them seems fully to have realized the subtlety and depth of her art, nor the perfection she brought to the novel form, which was to prove the chief vehicle of imaginative expression of the Victorian age. This is partly intelligible if we remember that she also culminated the eighteenth century art of fiction, and her six novels show some typically eighteenth-century assumptions about society and about attitudes to human nature. The Victorians abandoned and often despised many of these assumptions, which involved a static view of the social order while they were deeply preoccupied by change, and an ironic, illusionless conception of human nature which they were apt to interpret as moral shallowness or cynicism. Cynicism is indeed the charge which many Victorians would have made about many of our own attitudes, and in this respect our temper of mind is closer to Jane Austen's than it is to theirs; this is perhaps the principal reason why most of the valuable Jane Austen criticism has been produced in the last half century. But in regard to her static view of society, it is by no means the case that she was incapable of any other: I end this book by suggesting that had she lived the normal term, she might have become the first of the great Victorian novelists.

Yet this would not necessarily have meant that we should now admire her later work even more than her earlier. What has caused critics of the twentieth century to recognize the true greatness of the work which she accomplished is a sense of its unusual modernity. This is an effect of the alertness of her consciousness. Whatever our terrible shortcomings, we have learned from our characteristic thinkers—our psychologists, anthropologists, and sociologists—that survival depends on how well we can understand ourselves, and that our understanding depends on what we can observe, on how well we can interpret the evidence, and on how far we can relate the different categories of evidence to one another. The novelists have had an important part in forming this modern consciousness because they give us an image of social man in which we can imaginatively participate, not merely facts available only to our analysis. Jane Austen was the first in our language to understand this novelistic function with full clarity, and few have understood it better since.

Part One
Biographical Background

Chronological Table

1784	Jane and Cassandra sent to Abbey School, Reading, under Mrs Latournelle.	Cowper: *The Task* Death of Samuel Johnson
1785	Education continued informally at home. Learns French, some Italian, the piano, and reads English literature extensively.	
1787	Family theatricals (including *The Rivals*) in the Steventon barn. Jane begins to write sketches.	
1789		Beginning of French Revolution
1790	*Love and Freindship*.	Edmund Burke: *Reflections on the French Revolution*
1791	Edward marries Elizabeth Bridges. The *History of England*.	Thomas Paine: *Rights of Man* I
1792	James marries Anne Mathew. *Evelyn, Catharine*, etc.	Paine: *Rights of Man* II Mary Wollstonecraft: *A Vindication of the Rights of Woman*
1793		William Godwin: *Political Justice* War with France; French Reign of Terror under the Jacobins
1794	Elizabeth de Feuillide's husband guillotined in France. Jane working at *Lady Susan*.	Mrs Radcliffe: *The Mysteries of Udolpho* Godwin: *Caleb Williams*
1795	Death of James's first wife. Cassandra engaged to Thomas Fowle.	The Directory takes over the government of France
1796 –8	Jane working at *Elinor and Marianne* (later *Sense and Sensibility*); *Susan* (later *Northanger Abbey*); *First Impressions* (later *Pride and Prejudice*).	Burney: *Camilla* Robert Bage: *Hermsprong* William Wordsworth and Samuel Coleridge: *Lyrical Ballads*

1797	Death of Cassandra's fiancé, Thomas Fowle. James marries Mary Lloyd. Edward inherits Kent and Hampshire estates from Thomas Knight. Henry m. Elizabeth de F.	
1799	Mrs Austen's sister-in-law, Mrs Leigh Perrot, arrested for shoplifting in Bath. Acquitted.	
1800	Jane seems to have had a brief romance with a gentleman met at Sidmouth; he dies soon after.	Death of Cowper Maria Edgeworth: *Castle Rackrent*
1801		Edgeworth: *Belinda*
1802	Jane receives a proposal of marriage from Harris Bigg Wither; she accepts him but withdraws the next morning.	Peace of Amiens Walter Scott: *Minstrelsy of the Scottish Border*
1803	Sells the ms of *Northanger Abbey* for £10 to Crosby in expectation of publication.	War with France renewed
1804	Visits Lyme Regis. Begins *The Watsons* (perhaps an early draft of *Emma*). The death of Mrs Lefroy, Jane's best friend.	Napoleon declared Emperor of France
1805	Death of Jane's father. Mrs Austen and her daughters move to Southampton.	Battle of Trafalgar Scott: *The Lay of the Last Minstrel*
1807	Charles marries Fanny Palmer.	Madame de Staël: *Corinne* Crabbe: *The Parish Register* Abolition of slave trade
1808		Scott: *Marmion* Beginning of Peninsular War
1809	Mrs Austen and her daughters move to Chawton in Hampshire, on Edward's estate. Crosby returns the unpublished ms of *Northanger Abbey*.	Hannah More: *Coelebs in Search of a Wife* Death of Sir John Moore in Spain
1810		Scott: *The Lady of the Lake* Crabbe: *The Borough*

4

1811	*Sense and Sensibility* published: 'a novel by a Lady'.	
1812	*Pride and Prejudice* sent to publishers; *Mansfield Park* begun.	Byron: *Childe Harold* Crabbe: *Tales*; Napoleon invades Russia
1813	*Pride and Prejudice* published; well received. Jane's last visit to Edward at Godmersham.	Southey: *Life of Nelson*
1814	*Mansfield Park* published; *Emma* begun.	Restoration of the Bourbons in France Scott: *Waverley*
1815	Jane Austen in London with Henry; the Prince Regent orders his librarian, James Clarke, to give her every attention. *Emma* consequently dedicated to the Prince Regent.	Battle of Waterloo Scott: *Guy Mannering*
1816	*Emma* published. Walter Scott's essay on Jane Austen in the *Quarterly Review*.	Byron: *The Prisoner of Chillon* Scott: *The Antiquary*; *Old Mortality*
1817	*Persuasion* completed and 'put upon the shelf for the present'. Jane Austen, having contracted Addison's disease, moves to Winchester for better medical attention. Dies on 18 July.	John Keats: *Poems*
1818	Publication posthumously of *Northanger Abbey* and *Persuasion*.	Mary Shelley: *Frankenstein*

Silhouettes of Jane Austen's parents,
the Reverend George Austen and his
wife, formerly Cassandra Leigh.
Profiles in silhouette were in Jane
Austen's day the equivalent of the
modern photographic portrait.

1 Character and Family Background

One of the most misleading facts that are widely known about Jane Austen is that her life was what is called 'uneventful'. Her biography can indeed be quickly summarized.

She was born on 16 December 1775, at her father's rectory at Steventon in Hampshire, the seventh in a family of eight children. She lived with her parents until the death of her father in 1805, and then with her mother until the year of her own death. The household moved from Steventon to Bath in 1801, from Bath to Southampton in 1806, from Southampton to the Hampshire village of Chawton in 1809. Every change of address represents, on the whole, a downward social direction. She died on 18 July 1817, in Winchester, where she and her sister Cassandra had taken lodgings so as to be near her doctor. Her death seems to have been due to a then obscure illness called Addison's Disease. She visited other places, including London and a number of country houses, but she scarcely left the south of England. She and her sister attended boarding-schools at Oxford, Southampton and Reading when she was between the ages of seven and nine, but she received most of her education at home. She never married, though she received at least one proposal; she may have had at least one love affair, but little is known about it except that it was not connected with the proposal. She seems to have had no direct relationships with any of the famous men and women of her time, unless we call the royal invitation to dedicate one of her novels to the Prince Regent a direct relationship. The memorable events seem to have been the publication of the novels: *Sense and Sensibility* (1811), *Pride and Prejudice* (1813), *Mansfield Park* (1814), *Emma* (1815); after her death, *Northanger Abbey* and *Persuasion*, in December 1817.

What, apart from the novels, could appear more commonplace? And for that matter what could be more commonplace than the events in those novels? And yet, as novels, they are so far from being ordinary or commonplace that few by other writers contain so much quickness of life so well sustained. We do not judge them, of course, by the amount of shock they produce in the nervous system, but by their luminousness. Correspondingly, the facts about Jane Austen's life illuminate her art only in so far as we seek in them what is illuminating, not what is glamorous or startling.

To begin with the large family of which she was a member. The father, George Austen, came from stock which dated itself back to the class of medieval clothiers which were known as 'the Grey Coats of Kent'—'a body so numerous and united that at county elections whoever had their vote and interest was almost certain of being

elected', or so a local historian, Hasted, asserted. They continued to flourish as a class into the seventeenth century, and the same historian states that they possessed 'most of the landed property in the Weald, insomuch that almost all the ancient families in these parts, now of large estates and genteel rank in life, and some of them ennobled by titles, are sprung from ancestors who have used this great staple manufacture, now almost unknown here'. In fact, they provided the varied, vigorous stock which by the eighteenth century was proliferating from commerce into the main professions—the Church, the fighting services, the law—as well as into landowning. In short, they became the gentry, whose upper reaches joined the aristocracy and whose lower ones were among the attorneys, apothecaries and surgeons of the country towns. It was an exceptionally vigorous class, at the height of its vitality if not yet of its influence in George Austen's lifetime. The characteristic vice of its members might be snobbery, since they had the best opportunities for social advancement; their corresponding virtue was a combination of practical force with cultured refinement: an awareness of the commonplace tasks of daily living and of the hardships of the poor, as well as sensitiveness to the life of the mind. This was the class which was to be the subject of Jane Austen's novels.

George Austen's father belonged to its lower levels: he was a Tonbridge surgeon, and a comparatively poor man; moreover, both the parents died when George was still a boy. However, a rich uncle paid for his education, and he later gained a scholarship to St John's College, Oxford. He was a schoolmaster for a time, and then became a Fellow of his college. In Oxford he was known as 'the handsome Proctor'. Besides his good looks, all accounts represent him as a scholarly, affectionate, sweet-tempered man. He took orders in 1760, and another well-to-do relative, Thomas Knight of Godmersham House in Kent, presented him with the living of Steventon. In 1764, he married Cassandra Leigh.

Her family was more eminent than his. She had titled relatives, an ancestor who had been Lord Mayor of London in the reign of Elizabeth, another who had given shelter to Charles I; her grandfather had been brother-in-law to the Duke of Chandos whose ostentation had possibly been satirized by Pope in a *Moral Essay*, and her uncle was Master of Balliol College, reputed for his wit. Like her husband she was handsome, and like her uncle she was witty; her great-nephew writes: 'She united strong common sense with a lively imagination, and often expressed herself, both in writing and con-

Godmersham Park. The mansion was owned by Mr Austen's cousin, Thomas Knight, who adopted the third son, Edward, and made him his heir. The Austen girls, especially Cassandra, spent long visits there.

versation, with epigrammatic force and point.' Her own term for it was 'sprack wit'. She seems to have been a woman of too much assurance to have had any pretensions, and was not afraid to be found 'busy with her needle' in the front room of the rectory, on to which the front door directly opened. But she may have been a good deal of a hypochondriac; in one letter, Jane writes: 'My mother continues hearty, her appetite and nights are very good, but her Bowels are not entirely settled, and she sometimes complains of an Asthma, a Dropsy, Water in her Chest and a Liver Disorder.'

Jane had five brothers and a sister older than herself, and a younger brother. She was the youngest to die, at the age of forty-two—a fact worth noting in view of the large infantile mortality of those days—although the second son, George, was permanently incapacitated by a mental illness which prevented him from living with the rest of the family; he is like a faint, sad ghost in the background of the otherwise happy and successful Austens. They were close in years, for the eldest, James, was born in 1765, and the youngest, Charles, in 1779; thus, since they seem also to have been united by strong affection, they were able to live as a well-knit community.

To understand what the Austen family was like it is worth trying to picture it between 1785 and 1790, at about the time Jane Austen began writing.

Jane and her only sister Cassandra, about two years the elder, came home from school for the last time in 1784 or 1785. The school was the second they had attended; from the first, which had moved from Oxford to Southampton, they were rescued when they fell ill of the 'putrid fever'; the aunt who fetched them died of the infection. The second school, at Reading, was attended a few years later by the future Mrs Sherwood who left an account of it. The Abbey School was kept by Mrs Latournelle who was without academic qualific- ations but had immense energy (in spite of a cork leg) and delighted in talk about the theatre. She also had the virtue of a high standard of cleanliness for her establishment. Since it seems that no one cared how the girls spent their time so long as they attended their morning classes, they must have had extensive freedom. Jane was no doubt happy if only because she was with Cassandra—'If Cassandra were going to have her head cut off', wrote Mrs Austen, 'Jane would insist on sharing her fate'—but it may have been Mrs Latournelle's enthusiasm for the theatre that impressed her most deeply there. From 1785 onwards the sisters must have received most of their education from their brothers, James and Henry, as well as from their father who (as Henry later reported) was 'not only a profound

Steventon Parsonage in which Jane Austen grew up, from a contemporary sketch. The house was pulled down in the 19th century.

scholar but [possessed] a most exquisite taste in every species of literature'. He had not sent his sons to school but had educated them himself.

James Austen-Leigh, whose memoir of his aunt was published in 1870, describes the Parsonage House (by then pulled down):

> The house itself stood in a shallow valley, surrounded by sloping meadows, well sprinkled with elm trees, at the end of a small village of cottages, each well provided with a garden . . . It was sufficiently commodious to hold pupils in addition to a growing family, and was in those times considered to be above the average of parsonages; but the rooms were finished with less elegance than would now be found in most ordinary dwellings. No cornice marked the juncture of wall and ceiling; while the beams which supported the upper floors projected into the rooms below in all their naked simplicity, covered only by a coat of paint or white-wash . . . On the south side the ground rose gently, and was occupied by one of those old-fashioned gardens in which vegetables and flowers are combined, flanked and protected on the east by one of the thatched mud walls common in that country, and over-shadowed by five elms.

It was in fact more of an enlarged cottage than a mid-Victorian rector would care to live in, but it was a homely, unpretentious environment, spacious enough to accommodate a large household of young people. A friend, quoted by James Austen-Leigh, gives a glimpse of it as it was in 1788:

> With his sons (all promising to make figures in life) Mr Austen educates a few youths of chosen friends and acquaintances. When among this liberal society, the simplicity, hospitality and taste which commonly prevail in affluent families among the delightful valleys of Switzerland ever recur to my memory.

By 1787 or 1788, however, the household was often smaller. James had become a Fellow of his father's Oxford college; Edward had been adopted as his heir by the Thomas Knight who had presented the living of Steventon to Mr Austen; Francis attended the Royal Naval Academy at Portsmouth; Henry, Jane's favourite, entered St John's College in 1788. Only the little brother, Charles, was permanently at home. Thus the girls were able to occupy two rooms on the first floor: a bedroom and a sitting-room which a niece remembered as furnished with a 'common-looking carpet with its chocolate ground, and painted press with shelves above for books' (including Dodsley's *Collection of Poems* and Richardson's *Clarissa*), Jane's desk and piano, Cassandra's drawing materials, and an oval looking-glass between the windows.

The brief catalogue of furniture indicates the sisters' indoor occupations, but they did not share their brothers' outdoor ones of riding, hunting and shooting. The letters (of which none survives earlier than 1796) show at least a normal interest in clothes and occupation with household work; they walked in the countryside, but the times were rough and a girl did not go far alone. Later there were frequent visits to the houses of friends and relatives; there were periodic balls in the neighbourhood, and Jane was fond of dancing, but in the 1780s she would have been too young to attend them. A distinctive Austen amusement in which they all shared was the performance of plays; these were acted in a neighbouring barn in the summertime, and in the parsonage dining-room in the winter.

These amateur dramatics were stimulated by a lively and pretty cousin, Eliza de Feuillide, who sometimes stayed with the Austens. She was the daughter of Mr Austen's sister, and had been born in India; her godfather was the famous Warren Hastings, whose son had been the first of Mr Austen's pupils, although he must have been principally Mrs Austen's care, since he came to them in infancy and died in early childhood. Elizabeth, on the death of her father, had been taken to Paris to complete her education; there she married the Comte de Feuillide who was guillotined in 1794, and in 1797 she was to marry Jane's brother Henry. She and her husband came to England in 1786 so that her child could be born here. After a season at Tunbridge Wells, where she induced the local theatre to put on Garrick's *Bon Ton* and Mrs Cowley's *Which is the Man,* she spent Christmas at Steventon, where the same plays were performed. She tried to induce another cousin, Philadelphia Walter, to join the party on condition that she took part, for 'my Aunt Austen declares she has not room for any idle young people'. She promised 'a most brilliant party and a great deal of amusement, the house full of company, frequent balls'.

All, or nearly all, the positive evidence shows the Austens to have been lively, active, happy, united. Possibly, most of the evidence to the contrary was suppressed: one remembers how very little is known of the second son, George, and the destruction of many of Jane Austen's letters. Those that survive contain gaily critical references to members of her family, but very few censorious ones. An exception is a passing mention in a letter of her eldest brother James in 1807:

> I am sorry & angry that his Visits should not give one more pleasure; the company of so good & so clever a Man ought to be gratifying in itself;—but his Chat seems all forced, his Opinions on many points too much copied from his Wife's, & his time here is spent I think in walking about the House & banging the doors, or ringing the bell for a glass of water.

Unlike the third brother, Edward, he was not 'a man of business', but next to his sister he seems to have had the most literary proclivities of the family, and while at Oxford he edited and largely wrote a periodical called *The Loiterer*—probably on analogy with Addison's *Spectator*. He became rector of Steventon on the retirement of his father. Edward inherited Thomas Knight's estate at Godmersham, and was knighted in 1812. Henry, the most attractive, versatile, and unstable of the brothers, hankered first after a military career and became Captain and Adjutant of the Oxford Militia; then he became a banker, but went bankrupt in 1816, and he ended as a country clergyman like James. He seems to have been charming, impulsive, a winning conversationalist, and resilient in misfortune; 'his Mind is not a Mind for affliction', Jane wrote when his first wife died. 'He is too Busy, too active, too sanguine.' It was he who left the first memoir of his sister, which he prefaced to the 1818 edition of *Persuasion*. The remaining brothers, Francis and Charles, both entered the navy and both rose to become admirals.

The Reverend George Austen died in 1805. He was not to know that three of his sons were to reach ranks of distinction, still less that he had a daughter of genius; but, always excepting the son called after him, he must have felt proud and hopeful of his family. The careers of his sons are representative: the strong stock of the Grey Coats of Kent had once been masters of the Weald; the same stock were now among the leaders of the nation. The Austens may or may not have always been so happy and united as biographers lead us to suppose, but it is clear that the family was always positive in its values and expectancies, both of themselves and of one another. They seem not to have been extraordinarily ambitious and they were certainly not rapacious, but they were proud and had a strong sense of their own dignity: qualities which make for success.

In one respect, however, his daughters did not fulfil expectations: neither of them ever married. This was evidently not because they were unattractive. As a child, Jane made a disagreeable impression on one cousin, Philadelphia Walter, but this may have been because, as she later said of herself in childhood, she was extremely shy. Philadelphia describes her in 1788 as 'not at all pretty and very prim, unlike a girl of twelve'. In 1807 Jane herself writes in a letter of the children she knew:

> What is become of all the Shyness in the World?—Moral as well as Natural Diseases disappear in the progress of time, & new ones take their place.—Shyness & the Sweating Sickness have given way to Confidence & Paralytic complaints . . . Our little visitor has just left us, & left us highly pleased with her;—she is a nice, natural, openhearted, affectionate girl, with all the ready civility which one sees in the best Children in the present day;—so unlike

anything that I was myself at her age, that I am all astonishment and shame.

The charm of children (as of older people) depends, of course, on how much at ease they feel in the company they are keeping. Jane Austen herself was clearly very good with children: her niece Caroline was to write in her short memoir 'As a very little girl I was always creeping up to aunt Jane and following her whenever I could, in the house and out of it . . . Her first charm to children was great sweetness of manner. She seemed to love you, and you loved her in return.' Her nephew recorded that 'We did not think of her as being famous; but we valued her as one always kind, sympathizing, and amusing.' (*Memoir*)

By 1791 she was evidently overcoming her childish gaucherie, for her cousin Eliza de Feuillide writes in a letter of her and Cassandra that they are 'very much grown . . . and greatly improved as well in manners as in person . . . two of the prettiest girls in England'. As children, Jane and Cassandra must have suffered from the deprivation of the outdoor activities of which their brothers were fond; they probably cultivated indoor occupations of reading, drawing, music and writing to what would now be considered excess. Their native vitality was brought out as they came out into society. Her nephew wrote this description of Jane as she was in her thirties:

> In person she was very attractive; her figure was rather tall and slender, her step light and firm, and her whole appearance expressive of health and animation. In complexion she was a clear brunette with a rich colour; she had full round cheeks, with mouth and nose well formed, light hazel eyes, and brown hair forming natural curls close round her face. If not so regularly handsome as her sister, yet her countenance had a peculiar charm of its own to the eyes of most beholders. (*Memoir*)

He also recalls that in family opinion 'Cassandra had the *merit* of having her temper always under her command, but that Jane had the *happiness* of a temper that never required to be commanded'. The devotion of the two sisters to each other lasted throughout their lives. Cassandra wrote in a letter after Jane's death: 'She was the sun of my life . . . I loved her only too well, not better than she deserved, but I am conscious that my affection for her made me sometimes unjust and negligent to others.'

Jane Austen's own personal affections were certainly among the strongest influences upon her, and they extended beyond her sister. The death of her friend Mrs Lefroy by a fall from her horse was one of the major bereavements of her life, and four years later she wrote the only serious poem that has come to light in her writings to commemorate it.

When we look further, into her deepest beliefs and opinions, much has to be inferred—for instance, her religion.

2 Religion

There were two principal styles of clergyman working in the Church of England in Jane Austen's lifetime. The first, which we may call the 'Establishment' kind, saw their profession in the same light as any other profession. A young man from the university took orders without evidence of spiritual vocation, and received his parish—his 'living'—from a landowner in whose gift it was, and who was likely to be at least equally indifferent. The other kind were designated 'Evangelicals', because they were evangelists who tried to reach the hearts of their parishioners. Whereas the Establishment clergy took the salvation of their parishoners' souls for granted, so long as they were church attenders and paid their tithes, the Evangelicals believed that it was their calling to bring home to their congregations a consciousness of their sinfulness and of their need for regeneration. Only when the preacher reached and stirred up the emotions of his listeners was he really doing his work, and the converted peasant meant more to the Evangelical than the unconverted landlord, however generous his patronage. For the Establishment clergy, on the other hand, this emotion-stirring meant 'enthusiasm'—a word which, at least in the earlier eighteenth century, had connotations resembling 'emotionalism' or even 'fanaticism' today. For the Establishment, Evangelicalism was vaguely subversive of society and dangerous to reason; it was at least ridiculous. The distinction between the two kinds of clergy goes back to the beginnings of the Church of England at the Reformation, but in the eighteenth century the Evangelicals derived their inspiration most from John Wesley (1703–91). Wesley had been forced out of the Church into his own Methodist movement, but his influence remained strong within it.

It is easy nowadays to be contemptuous of the eighteenth-century style of Establishment clergyman, but in fact he was not necessarily either insincere or useless. In practice, the value of such a clergyman—and Jane's father and two clerical brothers were both of this kind—depended not so much on his beliefs, though there is no reason to suppose that they were not genuine believers, as on his social conscience and his understanding of his parishioners. His understanding would in turn depend on the closeness of his relationship with them, and here the system may have had advantage just where it may seem to be most open to criticism. The clergy were paid by tithes based on their parishioners' produce. The method at least had the merit of bringing the parson's material interests close to theirs, as the diary of the eighteenth-century Parson Woodforde illustrates, and this would be particularly true if the parsonage, as was the case at Steventon, had a farm attached to it. A country clergyman, at least in a conservative rural area like Steventon, probably had much closer natural affiliations with his parishioners than his counterpart has now.

Jane Austen and the Clergy

How did Jane Austen see the class of clergy, so closely associated with her own background? Something can be deduced from her novels and letters. It is easy to forget that Henry Tilney of *Northanger Abbey* is a clergyman, but this was the earliest written of the novels, when she probably took the profession more for granted. Mr Collins, in *Pride and Prejudice*, is a fool and also the supreme conformist, who declares, on receiving the living from Lady Catherine de Burgh, that 'it shall be my earnest endeavour to demean myself with grateful respect towards her Ladyship, and be ever ready to perform those rites and ceremonies which are instituted by the Church of England'. No priest ever paid deference to Caesar before God more ingenuously, though certainly not a few lived by the doctrine. In *Mansfield Park*, the worldly Mary and Henry Crawford have something very like the modern prejudice about eighteenth-century clergymen:

> I am not entirely without the means of seeing what clergymen are, being at this present time the guest of my own brother, Dr Grant. And though Dr Grant is most kind and obliging to me, and though he is really a gentleman, and I daresay a good scholar and clever, and often preaches good sermons, and is very respectable, *I* see him to be an indolent, selfish *bon vivant*, who must have his palate consulted in everything; who will not stir a finger for the convenience of any one; and who, moreover, if the cook makes a blunder, is out of humour with his excellent wife. To own the truth, Henry and I were partly driven out this very evening by a disappointment about a green goose, which he could not get the better of. My poor sister was forced to stay and bear it.

This is not the only attack she makes on what she clearly regards as a practically redundant profession. When Edmund Bertram, who is to be ordained, objects that the 'office' of clergyman 'has the guardianship of religion and morals, and consequently of the manners which result from their influence. No one can call the *office* nothing', she retorts that since 'one scarcely sees a clergyman out of the pulpit', they hardly mix enough among people to exercise such a huge function. Edmund replies that this may be true of London, but that it is not true of the great mass of rural parishes, and he winds up by claiming 'that as the clergy are or are not what they ought to be, so are the rest of the nation'. Mary has nothing to say to this, she is not fundamentally interested in the question. She wants to marry Edmund, and she wants to marry a man with a brilliant career; she does not want to be buried in the country; and in those considerations her interest begins and ends. It is characteristic of Mary that her contentions are commonly right as far as they go, but right for the wrong reasons.

Henry Crawford also assumes that a clergyman's life must be an easy one, confined to preaching on Sundays, and implies that a parish priest need not reside in his parish. Sir Thomas corrects him: 'Human nature needs more lessons than a weekly sermon can convey; and . . . if he does not live among his parishioners, and prove himself by constant attention their well-wisher and friend, he does very little for their good or his own.' The prescription sounds secular and paternalist, as though a country clergyman should perform services corresponding to those of a modern psychiatric social worker, marriage guidance counsellor and probation officer. And those no doubt, together with others nowadays carried out by alternative means, did correspond to the functions of a conscientious clergyman in the early nineteenth century.

Sheer conscientiousness, however, would not be enough; other factors would have to operate for a clergyman to officiate successfully. One of these, in rural parishes of pre-industrial England, was the passive acceptance of the clergyman and of churchgoing as immemorial traditions in village life. In George Eliot's *Silas Marner*, published in 1861 but set in 'the early years in this century', the Warwickshire village woman, Dolly Winthrop, recommends the therapeutic value of church-going to Silas, who, as an ex-dissenter, has never been inside a church:

> If you've niver had no church, there's no telling the good it'll do you. For I feel so set up and comfortable as niver was, when I've been and heard the prayers, and the singing to the praise and glory o' God, as Mr Macey gives out—and Mr Crackenthorpe saying good words, and more partic'lar on Sacramen' Day; and if a bit o'trouble comes, I feel as I can put up wi'it, for I've looked for help i' the right quarter, and gev myself up to Them as we must all gev up to at the last; and if we'n done our part, it isn't to be believed as Them as are above us'ull be worse nor us are, and come short o'Their'n.

Her use of the plural, George Eliot explains, is 'only her way of avoiding a presumptuous familiarity' with God, but it suggests also

Walcot Church in Bath. Jane Austen's parents were married here, and her father lies buried in the churchyard.

her deference for and expectations of the whole religious system and her social superiors who are the earthly controllers of it. It was when they ceased to play their part—when the continuity was broken—that resentment began and a different sort of spirit, such as the evangelical one, might break in. When the poet-clergyman George Crabbe (whose verse the young Jane so much enjoyed that she declared her readiness to marry him should he be disengaged) absented himself from his Leicestershire parish for a long period, his parishioners fell under the influence of evangelical preachers who took his place without always residing in the village. In consequence, his relations with his parishioners cooled, although (in the words of his son) 'he was ever ready to help and oblige them all by medical and other aid to the utmost extent of his power. They carried this unkind feeling so far as to ring the bells for his successor, before he himself had left the residence.'

We do not know what relationships Jane Austen's father and brothers had with their parishioners; from negative evidence, we may infer that they were satisfactory, and it is fairly plain that they were clergy in the old tradition, and that the family tended to be hostile to evangelicalism because it was emotionally unbalancing to the judgment. In 1816 she writes to Cassandra: 'We do not much like Mr Cooper's new Sermons;—they are fuller of Regeneration & Conversion than ever—with the addition of his zeal in the cause of the Bible Society.' On the other hand she did not despise emotion as such. Of another preacher she writes: 'He gave us an excellent sermon—a little too eager sometimes in his delivery, but that is to *me* a better extreme than the want of animation, especially when it evidently comes from the heart as in him.' In 1809, lightheartedly she admits to prejudice against Hannah More's moralizing novel, *Coelebs in Search of a Wife*, before she had read it: 'I do not like the Evangelicals.' In general one gets the impression from her letters that she disliked ostentatious emotion and explicit moralizing, both of them characteristic of the evangelical cast of thought, but that she admired deep and spontaneous feeling and required moral conviction of the kind she called 'religious principle'.

From one letter, written in 1814, the year in which *Mansfield Park* was published, one learns rather more. The letter is addressed to her favourite niece, Fanny, and it is about a young man whom Fanny cannot make up her mind to marry:

And as to there being any objection from his *Goodness*, from the danger of his becoming even Evangelical, I cannot admit *that*. I am by no means convinced that we ought not all to be Evangelicals, & am at least persuaded that they who are so from Reason and Feeling, must be happiest & safest.—Do not be frightened from the connection by your Brothers having most wit. Wisdom is better than Wit, & in the long run will certainly have the laugh on her side; & don't be frightened by the idea of his acting more strictly up to the precepts of the New Testament than others.

The favourable tone about evangelicalism suggests a change of heart since 1809, but one remembers that the aspersions on Mr Cooper's evangelical sermons were written in 1816. More probably she is writing now in a more serious, considering spirit than usual. At all events the passage is interesting for two reasons. The first is that it suggests an epitome of *Mansfield Park*, in which Fanny's goodness and feeling, in alliance with Edmund's reason and principle, enable him to escape the enticements of Mary Crawford's wit. The second interest arises from the characteristic late eighteenth-century vocabulary: reason connoted a high value in the century which came to be designated the Age of Reason, and so did wit; feeling, in its later years, was increasingly brought to bear against the callousness and inhumanity which overvaluation of reason and wit was apt to produce. Wisdom and goodness have, of course, more ancient and universal connotations, and are primal biblical virtues. It was natural to eighteenth-century moralists to use such abstractions with far greater assurance than we do; it was the distinction of the novelists, and notably of Jane Austen, to give them flesh and blood.

In the end, the most that we can infer from Jane Austen's letters about her attitude to religion is that her faith was positive and important to her, but inclined to be conservative (if we can think of evangelicalism as 'progressive') and reticent, though I shall later try to demonstrate that *Mansfield Park* is fundamentally a religious novel. It is unsatisfactory, however, to leave the impression at this point that she seems to have divided her values into two sets: those that were 'religious', relating to conduct and social relationships, and the 'personal' set, having to do with the feelings of individuals for one another. Undoubtedly many people did make that kind of separation, hence part of the evangelical challenge. However, in her case we can establish a vital connection in the very important Austen virtue of 'candour'.

Candour

The word has shrunk in meaning since her day. Samuel Johnson defines it in his dictionary as 'sweetness of temper; purity of mind; openness; kindness'. Elizabeth Bennet defines it, addressing her sister Jane:

> 'With *your* good sense, to be so honestly blind to the follies and nonsense of others! Affectation of candour is common enough; one meets with it everywhere. But to be candid without ostentation or design, to take the good of everybody's character and make it still better, and say nothing of the bad, belongs to you alone.'

Jane Austen implies it, in one of the prayers that have survived among her compositions:

> Incline us, oh God! to think humbly of ourselves, to be severe only in the examination of our own conduct, to consider our fellow-creatures with kindness, and to judge of all they say and do with that charity which we would desire from them ourselves.

It seems to have been a strong virtue in herself, at least in her later years: her niece Caroline speaks of her complete absence of censoriousness when she talked of the neighbours. It is perhaps the central virtue in her novels.

In Jane Bennet of *Pride and Prejudice*, candour represents an unreserved outgoingness to people; a disposition not merely to do them justice, but to extend to them one's active sympathies. Yet at some point, candour must surely come into conflict with judgment: Elizabeth Bennet speaks half in exasperation, as though her sister has come by the virtue naturally but a little too easily; if she herself acquires it, it is at greater cost and perhaps at greater depth. Jane Austen herself, it seems likely, did not achieve the virtue without a struggle. Her readers have observed that her letters are full of a gay, sometimes irresponsible malice: 'Mrs Hall of Sherborne was brought to bed yesterday of a dead child, some weeks before she expected, owing to a fright. I suppose she happened unawares to look at her husband.' (1798)

This is a conspicuous example, and over much has in our own day been made of it, contained as it is in an intimate letter to Cassandra. But one gets to expect sardonic comments, some wittier than this and palpably more justified; of many, one is often unable to estimate their justification from ignorance of the context. It is certain that she had a strong inclination to sharp and even cruel humour, and that this runs counter to the general impression left by her relatives of her unusual sweetness of nature. The six novels are triumphs of sympathetic insight, but they also contain triumphs of caricature; the Austen method is to blend the two by manipulating varied and more or less subtle tones of irony. Their principal theme could be expressed as the education and chastening of the judgment.

3 Mysteries and Uncertainties

Tennyson, who was a strong admirer of Jane Austen, remarked, before the publication of the *Memoir* by James Austen-Leigh, that he was thankful that no more was known about her than about Shakespeare: sheer absence of data obviated the temptation to distracting and unverifiable speculation. Up to a point he was right: an imaginative writer lives in his works, and if a reader has only those by which to shape his judgment, he usually has nearly all that is essential. But Tennyson was not entirely right: if we knew more about Shakespeare's life, we might well be able to eliminate some of the teasing difficulties which obstruct the judgment of some of his plays. And not only does some biography afford clarification of a writer's work, but it can serve a valuable introductory function: if a writer lives in his work, we can only receive this life by feeling open to it; but it is difficult for many readers to escape an initial prejudice that if a writer is himself dead then the presumption is that his work is dead too. No logic supports this prejudice, but biography, by helping the reader to feel the writer's reality as a person, will do more than argument to dissipate it. Finally, whatever the advantages or disadvantages of possessing biographical knowledge, once the facts have been revealed they cannot be ignored: we have to read a writer to some extent in the light of what we know about his life, even if we end by deciding that what we know is of very little help to us in reaching our final estimate.

We now know a great deal more about Jane Austen than Tennyson did when he made the remark quoted at the opening of this chapter: not only has James Austen-Leigh's *Memoir* been published, but also other memoirs by those who recollected her or based on information derived from descendants of her family and friends. All this has been valuable in helping us to form a notion of her personality and experience of life, and in dispelling some false notions about her.

In particular, we know that the old notion of Jane Austen as the sheltered spinster, securely free from danger, squalor and tragedy, is largely a mistaken one. Some more than ordinary drama occurred to people closely connected with her. For instance, there was the arrest in Bath of her highly respectable aunt, Mrs Leigh Perrot, for shoplifting. Mrs Austen offered her the society of Cassandra and Jane in prison, but their aunt refused it. The case became a *cause célèbre*, and the aunt was eventually acquitted when it was discovered that she had been 'framed' with motives of blackmail. There was also the execution of Elizabeth de Feuillide's first husband, and the historic trial of Warren Hastings must almost have been a family drama in view of the Austens' connections with him. The bankruptcy of her brother, Henry, sudden and premature bereavements, the dangers undergone by her sailor brothers in the long wars, were other stresses on herself and her family. She knew, in fact, as much about the sad and anxious happenings of life as most people with a reasonably secure background do. But more important than such events is the evidence that her mental horizons must have been broader than usual, rather than more constricted. A girl whose great-uncle was Master of Balliol and famous as a wit, whose father and two of her brothers had attended the university, who had two more brothers in the navy and one active in the world of finance, who visited small and great country houses as well as London and lived for some years in the most fashionable inland resort in the country—such a girl had rather more than the usual experience of the world that surrounded her.

Against all this, it is true that if we compare her with the Victorian women novelists—George Eliot, Charlotte Brontë, Elizabeth Gaskell—her experience did have some limitations. She scarcely went outside the south of England; she is unique among the leading writers of her time in her isolation from personal contact with other leading writers; she probably never encountered serious social conflict and can scarcely have known much about the gigantic industrial changes in the Midlands and the north. Two other facts that seem to denote constricted experience—that she never married and never lived long apart from the family nucleus into which she was born—are doubtful evidence. Marriage might well have constricted her experience rather than enlarged it, especially if she had made a marriage of convenience rather than of love. We know that one evening she became engaged to the brother of one of her friends, and broke it off the next morning: the young man seems to have had every advantage except that she did not really love him. Family records suggest that she did have at least the beginnings of a real love affair, but that her lover died before they could become engaged. Cassandra may have remained unmarried for similar reasons: she was engaged to a man who died in the West Indies.

By inferences from her novels, and by literary detection, something can be inferred about her social and political opinions. Very interesting evidence, for instance, has been turned up by D. J. Greene. In an essay on 'Jane Austen and the peerage' (*Publications of the Modern Language Association of America*, vol. 68, 1953) he shows how the names of Jane Austen's characters correspond closely to names recurring in the annals of a group of great families connected, if distantly, with her mother's ancestral background. They include the Watsons, the title of one of her early experiments; the name of Wentworth, which is the surname of the hero of *Persuasion*; that of Woodhouse, surname of the heroine of *Emma*; Darcy, the surname

Sidney Gardens. When Mr Austen retired to Bath they lived in Sidney Place just opposite these pleasure gardens.

of the hero of *Pride and Prejudice*, and Fitzwilliam, the unmarried name of his mother. Moreover, all these names occur in a contemporary reference work on the peerage by one Arthur Collins, who, to judge by some of his published letters addressed to peers, seems to have been distinguished by the same fatuous obsequiousness before the nobility as characterizes Mr. Collins in the same novel. Particularly interesting are the names of Emma Wodehouse, by marrying whom a Wentworth united himself to the Woodhouse family in the thirteenth century, and Anne Wentworth, only granddaughter of Thomas, Earl of Strafford, the great minister of Charles I. Both, as Mr Greene points out, recall the two heroines with whom Jane Austen can personally be most easily connected, and the Strafford connection relates to her romantic conservative opinions evident in her youthful works, especially the *History of England*. The fact that Lord Fitzwilliam, at about the time she was writing her first version of *Pride and Prejudice*, was Viceroy of Ireland and a rather disastrous example of the arrogant Whig aristocracy which dominated English politics throughout the eighteenth century, is perhaps an indication of her Tory hostility to this oligarchy, expressed through her portrayal of Lady Catherine de Burgh, represented as the daughter and sister of a Lord Fitzwilliam. There is a more generally interesting suggestion of significance in Sir Walter Elliot's remark in *Persuasion*: 'One wonders how the names of our nobility become so common.' The Watsons are poor; Captain Wentworth in *Persuasion* was at first considered too poor and socially insignificant to marry a daughter of Sir Walter's; Emma Woodhouse has to divest herself of her social arrogance; Elizabeth Bennet (another surname in the aristocratic annals) has to conquer the respect of the arrogant Darcys and Fitzwilliams; the Dashwood sisters (still another such name) have to defy the haughty Ferrars. Jane Austen's conservatism was like Coleridge's in setting a strong value on continuity (witness Fanny Price in *Mansfield Park*). But it resembles his conservative philosophy in another way too: the intrinsic value of the person was always superior, for her, to the pretensions of mere status. The transformation of a person into an institution, and the attachment of respect to that, was for her unpardonable, as it was later for the much more radical George Eliot.

What we lack, when we look in her biography for illumination on her art, is any extensive record of her deeper inner experience, such as we have in the letters of Keats or the biography by a friend with insight, such as the life of Charlotte Brontë by Elizabeth Gaskell. Many of her letters were destroyed by her relatives, and the presumption is that these were the intimate, revealing ones, for those that remain, although their charm and interest grow with rereading, contain little of anything of the sort. In particular, the absence of any between 1801 and 1804, the period during which she is thought to have fallen in love, she lost her best friend, Mrs Lefroy, and Cassandra lost her lover, suggests the suppression of those written during painful crises.

The family reminiscences serve us little better. They either record tender, childish memories like those by her niece Caroline, or are almost formal tributes, like those by her brother Henry or her nephew James Austen-Leigh. The last has the additional disadvantage of being impregnated by the Victorian view of her as a sedative writer; it is a kind of portrait in twilight. Jane Austen, in one of her expeditions to London, played the game of looking for 'portraits' of her characters at exhibitions; she could find none of Elizabeth Bennet, whom she imagined to have become Mrs Darcy: 'I can only imagine that Mr D. prizes any Picture of her too much to like it should be exposed to the public eye.— I can imagine that he wd have that sort of feeling—that mixture of Love, Pride & Delicacy'. Her contemporaries seem to have had just such sentiments about her; the later generations, perhaps, were influenced by a more misguided piety.

What we do have, to take the place of more intimate records, are her 'juvenilia'—the fictional writings of her young girlhood. They are not discernibly biographical, but they are indirect records of the impact on her of her reading and of her growing experience and judgment of her personal relationships. Their characteristic tone is public and social, rather than intimate and private like the juvenilia of the Brontë family, but this fact reflects the period and the character of the Austen family rather than Jane Austen's personal inclination. Literature in the eighteenth century was a more social and sociable activity than it has become since: books were read aloud (there are a number of references to reading aloud in the letters) and not only Jane but other members of the family wrote for family amusement. James and Henry both contributed to *The Loiterer* which James edited at Oxford, and a nephew and two nieces sent specimens of their fiction to their aunt Jane for her criticism and advice. Thus the pieces in the Juvenilia are dedicated to members of her family and friends, and some were written for the entertainment of the youngest, Charles. Such as they are—and their quality is much above that of most youthful writing—they tell us something about how the mind of Jane Austen, the novelist, grew up.

4 Juvenilia

These writings date from 1787 to 1793, when Jane Austen was aged from eleven to seventeen. They include short novels, sketches, batches of fictional letters, playlets, and, written when she was sixteen, 'A History of England from the reign of Henry 4th to the death of Charles the first By a partial, prejudiced, and ignorant historian'.

Clearly, from its title-page, the History is a very lighthearted work, but just because it reads like a piece of spontaneous fun, we can infer something from it about the young Jane's response, not to history, but to the standards prescribed in her youth for the education of the feminine mind. This shows some signs of independent stirrings in the eighteenth century, and perhaps for that reason moralists and educationists were inclined to keep it in its place. Already in the *Spectator* of 1711, Addison shows signs of disapproval, if not of alarm:

> As our English women excel those of all Nations in Beauty, they should endeavour to outshine them in all other Accomplishments proper to the Sex, and to distinguish themselves as tender Mothers and faithful Wives, rather than as furious Partizans. Female Virtues are of a Domestick turn. The Family is the proper Province for Private Women to Shine in. If they must be showing their Zeal for the Publick, let it not be against those who are perhaps of the same Family, or at least of the same Religion or Nation, but against those who are the open, professed, undoubted Enemies of their Faith, Liberty, and Country.

Bound volumes of the *Spectator* were often in the hands of young ladies, and according to Henry Austen they were often in his sister's hands. Perhaps they were put there rather than chosen, for her only reference to the *Spectator* (in Chapter 5 of *Northanger Abbey*) is decidedly hostile. At all events, in her History she might be thumbing her nose at such a passage as this, and it is not only Addison and the *Spectator* that she is defying. History was considered a useful discipline for the feminine mind, but, wrote Lady Sarah Pennington in her *Unfortunate Mother's Advice to her Daughter*, it should be read 'not with a view to amuse, but to improve your mind'. Goldsmith's *History of England* was written for just such a public, and Jane Austen's is partly a take-off of his abridgement of his own work. Goldsmith prided

This artistic failure is unfortunately the only authentic portrait of Jane Austen. It is by her sister Cassandra.

himself on his impartiality—though he was certainly not impartial—and on his epitomizing style, which she emulates at least to the extent of leaving out almost all the facts. Addison might deplore 'Zeal for the Publick' in women, but the young Jane shows nothing else, being bent on 'proving' that certain causes and people were 'right' (specifically, the Yorkists, Mary Queen of Scots, and the Stuarts generally) and that everybody else (including that 'pest of Society' Queen Elizabeth) was detestably wrong. Lady Sarah might declare that the object of reading history was 'mind improvement', but Jane enjoys it as a means of letting her feelings have their way:

> I suppose you know about the wars between him [Henry VI] & the Duke of York who was of the right side; If you do not, you had better read some other History, for I shall not be very diffuse in this, meaning by it only to vent my Spleen *against*, & shew my Hatred *to* all those people whose parties or principles do not suit with mine, & not to give any information.

Love and Freindship

Writers like Mr Addison who tell you what you ought to feel, and how much, deserve mockery, for if you happen to hate Queen Elizabeth and adore Mary Queen of Scots, what business is it of his? On the other hand, Jane Austen was equally prepared to laugh at those who thought it right to live entirely by their emotions. A year before her History she wrote *Love and Freindship* (so spelt) as a burlesque on tales of passion and improbable romances generally. Again, the tale is just a joke, but the amount of comedy which she makes by burlesquing tales which are remote from reality, and from the self-absorption of self-infatuated characters obsessed by the keenness of their 'sensibilities', shows the direction which her artistic judgment is already taking. The hero meets the heroine after he has quarrelled with his father in Bedfordshire and run off to his aunt's house in Middlesex. But romantic writers contrive to get their heroes into romantic settings, and so—'tho' I flatter myself with being a tolerable proficient in Geography, I know not how it happened, but I found myself entering this beautifull Vale which I find is in South Wales, when I had expected to have reached my Aunts.' (Letter 6th). He has knocked at the door of the cottage where the heroine lives with her parents, and explains that his father had recommended a nice girl for him to marry. But of course a romantic hero must never accept his father's choice:

> 'No never exclaimed I. Lady Dorothea is Lovely and Engaging; I prefer no woman to her; but know Sir, that I scorn to marry in compliance with your wishes. No! Never shall it be said that I obliged my Father.'

'We all admired the noble Manliness of his reply.' He continued.

'Sir Edward was surprised; he had perhaps little expected to meet with so spirited an opposition to his will. "Where Edward in the name of wonder (said he) did you pick up this unmeaning Gibberish? You have been studying Novels I suspect." I scorned to answer: it would have been beneath my Dignity.' (Letter 6th).

Sheridan's plays were amongst those performed in the Austen barn, and no doubt Jane Austen remembered *The Rivals*, in which the hero has to disguise himself as his own poor rival to court the girl of his own and his father's choice, because she (also a great novel-reader) won't on principle consider him in his capacity as the suitor of her own guardian's choice.

The heroine of the novel of sensibility was always an epitome of all the perfections. Laura, one of the two heroines of *Love and Freindship*, sees no need to be reticent about her own:

> But lovely as I was the Graces of my Person were the least of my Perfections. Of every accomplishment accustomary to my sex, I was Mistress. When at the Convent, my progress had always exceeded my instructions, my Acquirements had been wonderfull for my Age, and I had shortly surpassed my Masters . . . (Letter 3rd)

She does, however, admit to one fault:

> A sensibility too tremblingly alive to every affliction of my Friends, my Acquaintance and particularly to every affliction of my own, was my only fault, if a fault it could be called. (Letter 3rd)

Egotists of the type that Laura caricatures were inclined to cultivate the literature of sensibility in order to find in it patterns of behaviour which gratified the image they had of themselves, as well as satisfying their antagonism to prevailing standards of social virtue:

> They said he was Sensible, well-informed, and Agreeable; we did not pretend to judge such trifles, but as we were convinced he had no Soul, that he had never read the Sorrows of Werter, & that his Hair bore not the slightest resemblance to Auburn, we were certain that Janetta could feel no affection for him, or at least that she ought to feel none. (Letter 12th)

Society was corrupt, and lived in cities, so that cultivators of sensibility sought the countryside, though there they were even more exposed to the painfulness of their endowment, as Sophia, Laura's co-heroine, finds:

> 'What a beautiful sky! (said I) how charmingly is the azure varied by those delicate streaks of white!' 'Oh! my Laura (replied she hastily withdrawing her Eyes from a momentary glance at the sky) do not thus distress me by calling Attention to an object which so

cruelly reminds me of my Augustus's blue sattin Waistcoat striped with white! In pity to your happy freind avoid a subject so distressing.' (Letter 13th)

Augustus has been imprisoned in Newgate. A dilemma arises for Sophia, for while as a woman of sensibility she is abnormally sensitive to his sufferings, for the same reason she cannot bear the sufferings that she will herself endure should she visit him there:

'Where am I to Drive?' said the Postilion. 'To Newgate Gentle Youth (replied I) to see Augustus' 'Oh! no, no, (exclaimed Sophia) I cannot go to Newgate; I shall not be able to support the sight of my Augustus in so cruel a confinement—my feelings are sufficiently shocked by the *recital*, of his Distress, but to behold it will overpower my Sensibility.' (Letter 10th)

To feel more on behalf of one's own sensibility than on behalf of one's lover must of course require a self-protecting regimen, but Sophia's sensibility is in the end too strong for her. The men of feeling were overinclined to lachrymosity; the women to fainting fits. Laura (like Fanny Burney's Cecilia) goes temporarily mad over the death of her lover, but Sophia goes into her final swoon:

'My beloved Laura (said she to me a few Hours before she died) take warning from my unhappy End & avoid the imprudent conduct that has occasioned it . . . beware of fainting fits . . . Though at the time they may be refreshing and Agreable yet believe me they will in the end, if too often repeated and at improper seasons, prove destructive to your Constitution . . . My fate will teach you this . . . I die a Martyr to my grief for the loss of Augustus . . . One fatal swoon has cost me my Life . . . Beware of swoons Dear Laura . . . A frenzy fit is not one quarter so pernicious; it is an exercise to the Body & if not too violent, is I dare say conducive to Health in its consequences—Run mad as often as you chuse; but do not faint—'
These were the last words she ever addressed me . . . It was her dieing Advice to her afflicted Laura, who has ever most faithfully adhered to it. (Letter 14th)

This seems to be a double parody: Sophia is not only the 'distressed heroine' of the novel of sensibility, but the dying mother of the eighteenth-century 'conduct book', bequeathing the essence of a lifetime's accumulated wisdom.

Portrait by Cassandra of Jane Austen's favourite niece, Fanny, daughter of her brother Edward

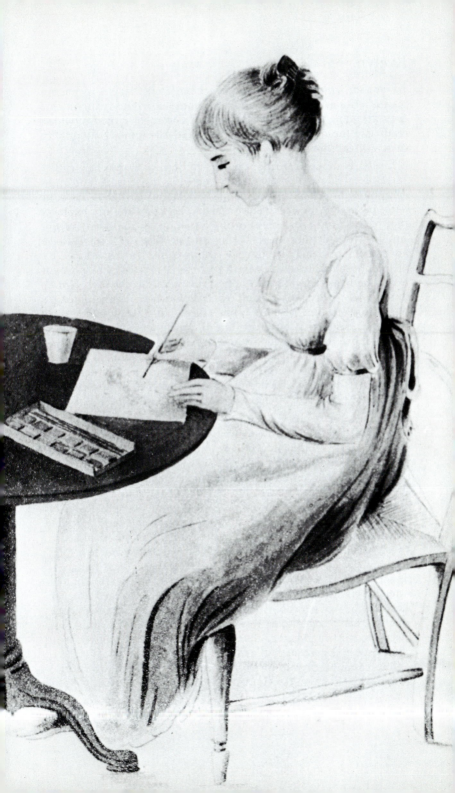

Evelyn

In 1792 she was writing stories in which burlesque mingles with more serious writing. As stories, they are less successful, but as experiments they are more interesting. The strangest of them is *Evelyn*, which reads like the description of a dream and has a fable-like quality such as dreams often convey.

Evelyn is supposed to be a village in Sussex. A traveller, called Mr Gower, comes upon it in the course of his journey and is so enraptured by it that he forgets his destination; his one desire is to settle in Evelyn for ever. The woman who keeps the inn explains that owing to 'the sweetness of the Situation, & the purity of the Air, in which neither Misery, Illhealth, or Vice are ever wafted', no houses are available, but she consoles him in his despair by mentioning a family which 'from a peculiar Generosity of Disposition would perhaps be willing to oblige you with their house'. Gower immediately calls upon Mr and Mrs Webb, who not only surrender their house to him without being asked, but also give him their beautiful daughter, who loves him devotedly at sight. Not only is no resistance offered to his wishes, but everything is done to make him secure in his own self-esteem. The perfect safety he is made to feel is reflected in the very symmetry of his house and garden; even the four white cows which graze the 'perfectly even and smooth' paddock are disposed 'at equal distance from each other'.

Fondness for regularity, smoothness, symmetry and security was one side of the eighteenth-century temperament; another side of it was a taste for sentiment, wildness, terror and mystery. The latter taste breaks into the story when Gower has got all he wants from the village. After some months of complete contentment, his wife accidentally reminds him of the purpose of the journey which he interrupted by handing him a rose. This recalls to him Rosa, his sister. She had been in love with the son of 'a noble lord' who had set his face against the match, and the young man had died at sea. When he stopped at Evelyn, Gower had been on his way to request a portrait of his sister's lover from the possibly penitent father. In shame, he now writes for news to his family, and learns that his sister too has died—of grief at his own long, unexplained absence. This bad news from the real world gives Gower an attack of gout; when he has recovered, he sets out for the noble lord's castle, now merely to discover whether that proud man is willing to give a kind of retrospective consent to the marriage.

The castle turns out to be a gloomy fortress characteristic of gothic tales of terror, like Horace Walpole's *Castle of Otranto*:

> The gloomy appearance of the old Castle frowning on him as he followed its winding approach, struck him with terror. Nor did

he think himself safe, till he was introduced into the Drawing room where the family was assembled to tea. Mr Gower was a perfect stranger to every one in the Circle but tho' he was always timid in the Dark and easily terrified when alone, he did not want that more necessary and more nobel courage which enabled him without a Blush to enter a large party of superior Rank, whom he had never seen before, & take his seat amongst them with perfect Indifference.

Again, touches of reality break in on the romantic fantasy. For the first time, we see Gower in opposition to something, and he begins to become a real person. On his own, he is a cowardly and superstitious little man, and his 'more necessary and more noble courage' is of course nothing but impertinence. Moreover, the straightforward politeness and rationality of the inhabitants of the improbable castle make Gower look silly as well as bad-mannered. When he puts his abrupt demand—'I wish to know whether the Death of this unhappy Pair has made an impression on your heart sufficiently strong to obtain that consent to their Marriage which in happier circumstances you would not be persuaded to give supposing that they were now alive'—his lordship, 'lossed in astonishment', merely points out that the demand is nonsensical, since 'to suppose them alive is destroying at once the Motive for a change in my sentiments concerning the affair'. Gower can only have recourse to downright rudeness. Calling his lordship 'a very vile Man', he takes horse again, and, 'almost distracted with his fears, and shutting his Eyes till he arrived at the Village to prevent his seeing either Gipsies or Ghosts, he rode on a full gallop all the way'.

At this point the story seems to have been continued by someone else—perhaps by a nephew or niece—and it is not worth pursuing. If we read it as a fable, she seems to have dropped it where the fable is complete. Gower is the typical self-ignorant egotist, without inner life, yet appreciative (like Laura in *Love and Freindship*) of what he believes to be the virtues of his own sensibility, and assertive, as she is, of what he conceives to be his rights in society, whose code of politeness commonly protects him from self-exposure. The village of Evelyn is his daydream of what life would be like if his wishes and his own notion of his merits were fully respected. But it would be rather dull, so he toys with the idea of himself as a romantic hero vindicating the rights of true love against the ogres of tyranny. But the real castle, real wilderness and real solitude, all terrify him, and the obdurate father of romantic fiction turns out to be a rational man whose politeness exposes Gower's heroism as impertinence, and whose logic exposes his heroic generosity as sentimentality. No authentic virtues can arise in a man who is 'easily terrified when alone'.

Catharine

To have feelings and opinions is our right; no one, not even the editor of the *Spectator*, can deprive us of them by merely asserting that they are wrong, or that we ought not to have any. But only rational argument can verify the justice of our opinions, and only 'candour' or openness to the feelings of others can verify the genuineness and real depth of our own. Jane Austen was later to centre her novels on some young girl who learns to distinguish the true from the false in herself by the gradual discovery that neither she nor those about her are really what she had at first assumed them to be. Among the fragments of 1792 is an unfinished novel, *Catharine*, which seems to have been her first serious attempt at such a theme. Catharine (also called Kitty) is an orphan, whose 'imagination was warm', and 'in her Freindships, as well as in the whole tenure of her Mind, she was enthousiastic'. The novel is subtitled 'The Bower', because she keeps a bower or arbour in the garden, where she reads her books and indulges her dreams, safe from her aunt, Mrs Percival, who brings her up. Mrs Percival scrutinizes her niece's conduct with such severity 'as to make it very doubtful to many people, and to Catharine amongst the rest, whether she loved her or not', although in fact she 'was most excessively fond of her, and miserable if she saw her for a moment out of spirits'. Mrs Percival's theme of conversation is that the nation is being ruined by contempt for propriety; she encourages her niece to read improving books such as Seccar's *Explanation of the Catechism*, and she dreads the bower as a certain source of the ailments to which she is sure the girl is susceptible.

Mrs Percival has smart relatives, the Stanleys, whom she has never dared to invite to stay because the family includes a grown-up son as well as a daughter, and she can only bring herself to do so when she hears that Edward Stanley is safely absent on a foreign tour. A ball is arranged at the neighbouring parsonage, to the delight of both girls, but on the day of it Catharine has the toothache, and so Mrs Percival and the Stanleys go to it without her. Then Catharine's toothache disappears, and she decides to follow them. Her preparations are just 'happily concluded by her finding herself very well-dressed and in high Beauty', when Edward Stanley drives up to the house and presents himself to her without at first explaining who he is and that he has had occasion to return unexpectedly from France. He insists on accompanying her to the ball, but Catharine, partly delighted and partly embarrassed by his unconventionality, protests that he is a stranger to their host as well as to herself.

'Oh! Nonsense, said he, I did not expect *you* to stand upon such Ceremony; Our acquaintance with each other renders all such

Prudery, ridiculous; Besides, if we go in together we shall be the whole talk of the Country—'

'To *me* replied Kitty, that would certainly be a most powerful inducement; but I scarcely know whether my Aunt would consider it as such—Women of her time of life, have odd ideas of propriety you know.'

He easily persuades her, and their entrance causes all the sensation they can both desire, especially to Mrs Percival, who is outraged. Camilla asks Catharine if she is in love with her brother:

'To be sure I am replied Kitty laughing, I am in love with every handsome Man I see.'

'That is just like me—I am always in love with every handsome Man in the World.'

The wording distinguishes their natures: Kitty is susceptible to men and knows it; Camilla dotes on the notion of being in love and is vain about it.

Catharine (Kitty) unintentionally steals the glamour of the ball from Camilla, and the rest of the fragment concerns its aftermath. Camilla sulks, Mrs Percival scolds, and Edward has to leave, though not before he has made an impulsive if indirect declaration of love. Catharine is a promising character, and one wonders why her story was not carried further. She is an ardent and (in the eighteenth-century sense) a candid girl, with great natural intelligence, but, thanks to her aunt's neurotic protectiveness, quite inexperienced in a world in which a young girl could not afford to be either vulnerable or ignorant—the perfect subject for startling adventures. However, it is probable that Jane Austen was already discarding romance for interest in what would have happened to such a girl in real life, and this would require a more substantial context for the central character than she was yet able to create.

Intervening Work

What looks like a long interval seems to divide the Juvenilia, of which Catharine is the last substantial example, written when she was sixteen, from the publication of *Sense and Sensibility* in 1811, issuing from Chawton, when she was thirty-five. In fact the gap was fairly well filled with work which was not published. She probably started *Elinor and Marianne*, the first and lost version of *Sense and Sensibility*, in 1794; *First Impressions*, the first and lost version of *Pride and Prejudice*, was begun, according to Cassandra, in 1796. Cassandra also says that the first version of *Northanger Abbey* (originally entitled *Susan*) was written in 1798–99. Between 1800 and 1805 she is known to have written the fragment called *The Watsons*, and perhaps the epistolary novel *Lady Susan*, although her nephew dates the latter ten years earlier. Thus we are left with a blank of six years (1805–11) when there is no evidence that she wrote any new work. A distinguished Jane Austen scholar, Q. D. Leavis, has expounded the theory that, just as Jane Austen is known to have developed *Sense and Sensibility* out of *Elinor and Marianne* and *Pride and Prejudice* out of *First Impressions*, so there is critical evidence that *Lady Susan* may have been worked into *Mansfield Park* and *The Watsons* into *Emma*. This might account for the apparently empty six years. The theory is not universally accepted, but it is consistent with the method and character of Jane Austen's art as we know it: it manifests highly wrought concentration and subtlety, and particularly in the way in which she developed her fine irony from what was in her adolescence a very broad caricature. Her writing life was a long assimilation of the social and moral climate in which she lived. We must now turn to the influences among her predecessors who contributed much to the character of this climate as well as to her own character as a writer.

Part Two
Literary Background

5 Augustan Sense and Sensibility

'Why, Sir, you find no man, at all intellectual, who is willing to leave London. No, Sir, when a man is tired of London, he is tired of life; for there is in London all that life can afford.'

SAMUEL JOHNSON (1709–84) reported in Boswell's Life

> God made the country, and man made the town:
> What wonder that health and virtue, gifts
> That can make sweet the bitter draught
> That life holds out to all, should most abound
> And least be threatened in the fields and groves?

WILLIAM COWPER (1731–1800) The Task, Bk I

He has more of Cowper than of Johnson in him, fonder of tame hares and Blank verse than of the full tide of human existence at Charing Cross.

JANE AUSTEN, Letter 90, 1813

Johnson was the greatest man of letters in the literary scene in the mid-eighteenth century; Cowper was the most eminent poet in the last quarter of it, before the rise of the Romantics. They dominated Jane Austen's youthful horizon, Johnson dying when she was eight years old, and Cowper when she was twenty-four. Johnson seems to have been the prose-writer she most admired, and Cowper (along with Crabbe, who was more her contemporary) her favourite poet.

The two men were in most ways strongly contrasted, as the quotations show. Not merely the sentiments but the wording of them shows the difference. Johnson's statement is quoted from his talk, but it has the terseness and definitiveness that characterizes all his utterances and makes so many of them epigrammatically memorable. Its tone has the forcefulness of strong feeling, and is equally characteristic in its touch of truculence and its effect of reined-in exuberance. Cowper's lines, in contrast, although the first has become a hackneyed commonplace, lack distinction; one would not be surprised to learn that some other hand had written them, Cowper merely incorporating them in his long meandering poem. No one else could have made Johnson's remark, in the way that he expressed it. Yet a few lines further, Cowper is writing lines as distinctive in his own way as Johnson's are in his:

> At eve
> The moonbeam, sliding softly in between
> The sleeping leaves, is all the light they wish,
> Birds warbling all the music.

This is the voice of the coming age: the voice of sensuous particularity as opposed to grand generality; of personal perception as opposed to social observation. It is the kind of writing which Jane Austen had in mind when she wrote in a letter: 'I could not do without a syringa, for the sake of Cowper's line. We talk also of a Laburnum', remembering 'Laburnum; rich/In streaming gold; syringa iv'ry pure'.

Merely from the quotations, one is not surprised that Johnson rejoiced in London's hurlyburly, where he had a wide circle of friends among the most eminent men and women of his time, whereas London was the scene of Cowper's first mental breakdown: he had to flee from it and immure himself till his death in country villages, dependent on the financial support of his family, although he was like Johnson in attracting admiring men and women among his close friends. They were different in other ways, not all of them to Cowper's disadvantage: his family was socially well-established, whereas Johnson was the son of a country bookseller and had no advantageous relatives. Cowper also was a good-looking man with naturally winning manners, whereas Johnson was personally awkward and disfigured. Finally, they were contrasted in their opinions: Cowper was a Whig and evangelical, whereas Johnson was a Tory and a conservative Anglican.

Yet they had strong resemblances of a more intimate kind, such that, had they met, it is easy to believe that they would have had a deep reciprocal respect. We know, indeed, from Cowper's letters, that he respected Johnson.

Both suffered severe fits of depression, Cowper's amounting to total despair. They were both strongly religious, but were obsessed with a sombre awe of death; they were both strongly critical of society and often of the same social vices, though with differences of emphasis. But the deepest quality that they shared may seem a relatively trivial one: both men abhorred affectation and cant, and had very strong affections; neither saw any reason to cultivate in himself an image that was more flattering than the truth as he felt himself to be; both, although in very different ways they must often have been very difficult to bear with, had that peculiar gift for friendship which consists in making a friend feel valued for being no other than he is.

It is this profound truthfulness of nature which gives their writings, dissimilar as they are, one quality in common making for endurance: one can always be sure that their opinions and feelings (in *writing*— Johnson was sometimes merely provocative in his talk) are fully meant. Of course they often made mistakes, and they had illusions—Cowper, very sick ones—but just as they never sought to disguise themselves from others, so they never tried to disguise reality from themselves. And this gave them still another quality in common: they were equally far from feeling or showing optimism about the human lot. It was not that they disbelieved that human beings could be happy—though Cowper had long periods in which he disbelieved that he could be—but they did not believe the human condition to be fundamentally a happy one.

Johnson's conception of the human condition is closer to Jane Austen's than is that of Cowper, for Cowper's belief in predestination—the doctrine that the individual can be saved only by divine grace, and that some individuals are predestined not to receive it—distorted his vision. Johnson believed that living is striving, and that he who strives hardest has the deepest satisfaction; in his own words (from *The Adventurer* 111): 'To strive with difficulties and to conquer them is the highest human felicity; the next is to strive and deserve to conquer them.'

Jane Austen's novels have so often been read as easy stories about easy living that it is worth pointing out a few of their characteristics that show them to be in line with Johnson's opinion. With a few significant exceptions, those of her characters who take life easily and lightly achieve success for themselves, are commonly just those who are shown to be shallowest, least likely to achieve enduring happiness for themselves or for others. Here one thinks particularly of the 'charming' young men, of Captain Tilney in *Northanger Abbey*, Willoughby in *Sense and Sensibility*, Wickham in *Pride and Prejudice*, Crawford in *Mansfield Park*, Churchill in *Emma*. Those who achieve at least the prospect of true happiness are often those who begin with the worst prospects and have to undergo the greatest difficulties. The obvious examples are the heroines of *Sense and Sensibility*, *Mansfield Park*, and *Persuasion*: Elinor Dashwood, burdened with a sense of responsibility, unlike her pretty, romantic sister Marianne; Fanny Price, burdened with the status of 'poor relation'; Anne Elliot, who has 'missed her chance' and lost her looks. There is also the 'hero' of *Sense and Sensibility*, Edward Ferrars, Elinor's lover, whose deep feelings and oppressed conscience dull any natural charm he may possess, in contrast to the facile and irresponsible Willoughby who is Marianne's lover. The two exceptions to the principle that happiness is more likely to be achieved from unpromising beginnings are Elizabeth Bennet and Emma Woodhouse, for both these begin their stories well pleased with their own charm and cleverness, and the second also possesses wealth and social status.

But these turn out to be the exceptions that prove the rule, for their advantages become disadvantages and they are brought low before they are able to stand firmly erect.

Portraits of Samuel Johnson by Joshua Reynolds; one informal showing his poor sight and expressing his strong but sombre character, the other more formal, expressing his role of the great man of letters. It was painted just after Johnson completed his Dictionary.

Johnson and Conservative Reason: 'Rasselas'

Samuel Johnson's measured pessimism is epitomized in his one short novel, *Rasselas*. It is not a novel in the usual sense, but a moral fable, which sets out to show, not that human beings cannot be happy, but that while they instinctively pursue happiness they are mistaken in supposing that it exists in any particular condition of life.

Rasselas is an Abyssinian prince, brought up according to the laws of the country in an isolated valley, barred by a huge gate from the outside world. He is himself unlikely to succeed, since he is the Emperor's fourth son, but the Happy Valley (much like Jane Austen's village of Evelyn) is a true paradise, where the princes 'lived only to know the soft vicissitudes of pleasure and repose, attended by all that were skilful to delight, and gratified with whatever the senses can enjoy.' Unlike Mr Gower of Evelyn, Rasselas is in no danger of being reminded of the outside world, since he has never known it, but he becomes sated with the ease and pleasure of his existence and yearns after it. 'Man', he decides, 'has surely some latent sense for which this place affords no gratification, or he has some desires distinct from sense which must be satisfied before he can be happy.'

After many months of self-deception, while Rasselas mistakes daydreaming about action for real action, he makes his escape. He is accompanied by his sister Nekayah, her friend and attendant Pekuah, and an aged poet-sage called Imlac, who has already travelled widely in the world and acts as their guide. They arrive in Cairo and sample the various conditions of life there and in the surrounding country. They find that the poor shepherds are ignorant and resentful, that the rich live in terror, that those in middle life, if unmarried, lead barren lives, and if married, lead lives of dissension; that those who seek society are full of envy and those who seek solitude are bored; that the philosphers are arid and vain, and the pleasure-seekers trivial. In short, they are unable to make any 'choice of life', since they find that each has its fatal and characteristic disadvantage.

About midway, the direction of the fable changes, from concern with our illusions about the search for happiness to concern with our illusions about the aversion of misfortune. The party visits the Great Pyramid, but Pekuah's superstitious terrors about its interior induce the Princess to allow her to remain outside. In consequence, she is carried off by a bandit. Nekayah is for a long time inconsolable, but to her vexation she finds that by degrees her sorrow wears off so that she has to force herself to think of her favourite. However, no efforts are spared to recover Pekuah, who is eventually restored in return for a ransom. It turns out that her captivity was no misfortune at all.

The bandit was no thug but a patriotic guerrilla leader against Turkish oppression who needs money for his cause, and he has been glad of Pekuah's company simply for the sake of a little intelligent conversation, since he has plenty of silly women to satisfy his sensual needs. She has been treated not merely hospitably but regally, to the extent that she at least might be supposed to have found the truly happy condition. However, it is not she who has been pursuing happiness so much as Nekayah, and it is not happiness but Nekayah, with whatever misfortunes, that she chooses.

Johnson brings out three points in this central episode. First, Pekuah, in trying to avoid an illusory disaster, causes a real one to befall her. Her situation is much like that of Catherine Morland in *Northanger Abbey*. Catherine expects impossible terrors from a gothic abbey, and is unaware that she is in the hands of a coldhearted bandit (disguised as a respectable retired general) who believes that he has made in her a rich capture for his son. But Catherine's real disaster turns out to be her good fortune, and so does Pekuah's; Pekuah is not only treated like a queen but returns to the princess a much more sensible woman—she has even had free tuition in astronomy. The third point Johnson makes is that Pekuah rejects her happy estate preferring a personal relationship.

The final episode in *Rasselas* is that of the mad astronomer, who has fallen victim to the agonizing delusion that he alone is responsible for the climate of the world, so that if he relinquishes his duties he will bring great calamities on mankind. Rasselas and his party manage to cure him of this needless burden of misery, which is in effect an allegory for the excessive anxiety with which overconscientious people see their responsibilities. At the end of the fable, Imlac and the astronomer are 'contented to be driven along the stream of life without directing their course to any particular port'. Nekayah dreams of a women's college, Pekuah of a convent, and Rasselas desires a little kingdom which he could govern ideally, 'but he could never fix the limits of his dominion, and was always adding to the number of his subjects'. However, 'of these wishes that they had formed they well knew that none could be obtained'.

The more serious moral comes in the penultimate chapter, when they visit the catacombs of the dead, a sojourn which causes them solemn reflections. At last—

> 'Let us return,' said Rasselas, 'from this scene of mortality. How gloomy would be these mansions of the dead to him who did not know that he shall never die; that what now acts shall continue its agency, and what now thinks shall think on for ever. Those that lie stretched before us, the wise and the powerful of ancient times, warn us to remember the shortness of our present state:

they were, perhaps, snatched away while they were busy, like us, in the *choice of life*.'

'To me,' said the princess, 'the *choice of life* is become less important; I hope hereafter to think only on the choice of eternity.'

Doctrinally, Johnson means that the human instinct to aspire to happiness is a religious one, and that wisdom teaches us that our expectation of happiness is the reflection of a promise, not for this world, but for the next. More practically, the lesson of the whole fable is that the pursuit of happiness and attempt to evade misfortune will only distract us from the realities in which we have to live. Life offers no assurances but constant surprises: we can foresee neither the true nature of our opportunities nor the consequences of our choices.

Johnson and the Art of the Novel

Yet the fact that we cannot predict the course of our lives does not mean, for Johnson, that we cannot order them. 'Truth', Imlac asserts in chapter XI, 'such as is necessary to the regulation of life, is always found where it is honestly sought.'

It is a statement which not only implies the possibility of and necessity for moral sincerity; it also assumes the possession of a reliable judgment which will recognize the truth when it is seen. In Essay number 4 of *The Rambler*, Johnson is specific about this:

> Some have advanced . . . that certain virtues have their correspondent faults, and therefore to exhibit either apart is to deviate from probability. Thus men are observed by Swift to be 'grateful in the same degree as they are resentful'. This principle, with others of the same kind, supposes man to act from a brute impulse, and pursue a certain degree of inclination, without any choice of the object; for, otherwise, though it should be allowed that gratitude and resentment arise from the same constitution of the passions, it follows not that they will be equally indulged when reason is consulted; yet unless that consequence be admitted, this sagacious maxim becomes an empty sound, without any relation to practice or to life.

Johnson is admitting that human beings are highly complex emotional organisms, but he says there is no point in making such an observation if we only mean by it that we are 'mixed up'; the problem of living is to make order from the muddle, and that is why we have a reasoning faculty.

In this essay, written in 1750, Johnson's subject is the new kind of fiction by Fielding, Smollett and Richardson, for which the previous decade had been so notable. He begins by observing that it is new because

Its province is to bring about natural events by easy means, and to keep up curiosity without the help of wonder: it is therefore precluded from the machines and expedients of the heroic romance, and can neither employ giants to snatch away a lady from the nuptial rites, nor knights to bring her back from captivity; it can neither bewilder its personages in desarts, nor lodge them in imaginary castles.

This he acknowledges to be an improvement, but he also considers that it entails an extra responsibility. No normal person would want to imitate a character in an old-fashioned romance; the character would be too improbable.

But when an adventurer is levelled with the rest of the world, and acts in such scenes of the universal drama, as may be the lot of any other man; young spectators fix their eyes upon him with closer attention, and hope by observing his behaviour and success to regulate their own practices.

It follows that the new fiction may be of greater moral efficacy than any mere preaching, but that if the novelist ignores his moral responsibilities, his work may be proportionately dangerous. So Johnson concludes:

There are thousands of the readers of romances willing to be thought wicked, if they may be allowed to be wits. It is therefore to be steadily inculcated, that virtue is the highest proof of understanding, and the only solid basis for greatness: and that vice is the natural consequence of narrow thoughts, that it begins in mistake, and ends in ignominy.

So Johnson believed that the nearer fiction came to life, the more it should serve the purposes of moral instruction. A novel that does not attempt moral discrimination is meaningless—'without any relation to practice or to life'; a novel which attempts to distinguish only brilliance—'men indeed splendidly wicked, whose endowments threw a brightness on their crimes'—is harmful, because it invites wrong emulation, and it is also false to the truth. Before we convict him of trying to tie the novel to a bishop's apron-strings, we need to take in this belief of his about the deep identification of truth with virtue. It recalls Jane Austen's warning to her niece: 'Wisdom is better than Wit, and in the long run will certainly have the laugh on her side'—for by wisdom she means what Imlac means by possession of the 'truth . . . necessary to the regulation of conduct'.

Leaving aside for the moment Johnson's notion of the novelist's duty, we can see that his moral viewpoint was certainly close to Jane Austen's. Among her characters, the Knightley brothers in *Emma* most closely embody his values. Boswell in his *Life* insists on Johnson's regard for truthfulness; George Knightley bases himself on the same regard, and despises Frank Churchill for his unmanly deceptions. When the volatile Boswell confessed that he sometimes professed opinions he did not hold, Johnson said: 'My dear friend, clear your *mind* of cant . . . you may *talk* in this manner; it is a mode of talking in Society: but don't *think* foolishly.' Analogously, when Emma makes up plausible arguments to justify her fantasy, Mr Knightley retorts, 'Better be without sense than misapply it as you do' (Chapter 8). Just as Johnson summed up the characters even of those he loved with a cool, judicious trenchancy, so, when someone pities Mr Weston for having had to surrender his son to Mrs Churchill, Mr Knightley sums up his friend's position with a very Johnsonian, disillusioned, yet just insight:

> '. . . You need not imagine Mr Weston to have felt what you would feel . . . Mr Weston is rather an easy, cheerful-tempered man, than a man of strong feelings; he takes things as he finds them, and makes enjoyment of them somehow or other, depending I suspect, much upon what is called *society* for his comforts, that is, upon the power of eating and drinking, and playing whist with his neighbours five times a week, than upon family affection, or anything that home affords.' (Chapter 11)

Yet even as clearsightedness about limitations in no way negated, for Johnson, his sense of obligation to others, so Knightley's sense of Mr Weston's tepidity of family feeling does not extenuate Frank Churchill's neglect of his father:

> 'There is one thing, Emma, which a man can always do if he chooses, and that is, his duty; not by manoeuvring and finessing, but by vigour and resolution. It is Frank Churchill's duty to pay this attention to his father.' (Chapter 18)

There is a vigour and warmth about the Knightley morality, combined as it is with the determination to see people as they really are, which quite vindicates it from any suspicion of restrictive primness or coldhearted smugness; and the same is to be said of Johnson's. They have the morality of strong mature minds which perhaps flourished best in the eighteenth century; it is not for nothing that it has been called the 'Age of Reason'.

Jane Austen did not agree with Dr Johnson merely in the sense that she modelled characters upon his; she was an engrained Augustan of his sort in the way that her style, like his, has the definition, balance and assurance which are themselves expressions of Augustan faith in clarity, judgment and good sense. Such a faith includes a clearsightedness about the incongruity between pretence and reality which makes irony a more prevalent tone in eighteenth-century writing than in any other. It is most conveniently observed in the openings of some of her novels, for instance that of *Northanger Abbey*, where she mocks at the assumptions behind the gothic romances, which succeeded the heroic romances alluded to by Johnson in *Rambler 4*:

> No one who had ever seen Catherine Morland in her infancy would have supposed her born to be a heroine. Her situation in life, the character of her father and mother, her own person and disposition, were all against her. Her father was a clergyman, without being neglected or poor, and a very respectable man, though his name was Richard, and he had never been handsome. He had a considerable independence, besides two good livings, and he was not in the least addicted to locking up his daughters. Her mother was a woman of useful plain sense, with a good temper, and, what is more remarkable, with a good constitution. She had three sons before Catherine was born; and, instead of dying in bringing the latter into the world, as anybody might expect, she still lived on— lived to have six children more—to see them growing up around her, and to enjoy excellent health herself. A family of ten children will always be called a fine family, where there are heads, and arms, and legs enough for the number; but the Morlands had little other right to the word, for they were in general very plain, and Catherine, for many years of her life, as plain as any.

It is a much lighter style than. Johnson's, particularly than his earlier style in *The Rambler*. But it has the same economy in two respects: first, in possessing a deliberate organization directed towards particular distinct effects; and, second, in that kind of clarity which keeps the reader's mind clear of what is *not* the writer's concern. Moreover, the conviction with which the limited point is made carries beyond its immediate reference. Johnson's literary criticism has the same virtues: the reader may wish him to take account of other issues, but at least he can be sure of the issues that Johnson is concerned with; he can also see that the other issues are not in Johnson's view at the moment, and that Johnson's point has inherent permanent validity. For instance, Johnson complains of *Lycidas*, Milton's elegy for Edward King, on account of the quantity of mythical references in it, that 'where there is leisure for fiction there is little grief'. The reader may feel that perhaps Milton was not after all mainly concerned with grief for King, but Johnson's point is nonetheless clear on his assumption that Milton *was* so concerned, and worth making because it makes a permanently valid objection to ornament for its own sake. So, in the opening of *Northanger Abbey*, Jane Austen makes clear her limited point that the word 'heroine' need not connote romantic extravagance, and that if it does, the character and her story are not likely to have much to do with real experience. Towards the end of her life, Jane Austen seems to have felt that the point was no longer worth making; that gothic novels did not invite attack in 1816 as they had done in 1803. But the passage retains its freshness, because its point carries beyond the ephemeral problem of the relevance to life of just one kind of fiction to the perennial one of the relevance of all fiction, and indeed of all art.

Yet, although there is a profound affinity between Jane Austen and Samuel Johnson, one can hardly suppose that she would have gone all the way with him in his *Rambler* essay. She would surely not have relished his assumption that the new realistic novels were 'written chiefly to the young'. But beyond this, Johnson, in his anxiety to protect these young seems to take no account of process, growth, and sensitizing in the development of a moral sense. Moreover, morally as well as physically a robust man, he may not have understood that more delicate temperaments might have different but not inferior insights, which could only be expounded by offsetting them to temperaments which seem much stronger, but in fact are weaker because they are more superficial. There are, in fact, aspects of Jane Austen which do not recall Johnson at all: there is a Fanny Price as well as a George Knightley. And in Jane Austen's background there is a Cowper influence as well as a Johnson one.

Cowper and Sensibility

Cowper's tragedy was his conviction that he was fundamentally isolated from God and man; it was a conviction that persisted despite his irreproachable life, the devotion of his friends, and his religious fervour. The pain of this isolation was increased by his being very much a man of his century, and consequently assuming man to be a social animal, requiring society for his fulfilment. In his own words:

> Man in society is like a flow'r
> Blown in its native bed. 'Tis there alone
> His faculties expanded in full bloom
> Shine out, there only reach their proper use.
> *(The Task: Winter Evening)*

As he saw himself in the society of his age, he was

> a stricken deer that left the herd
> Long since; with many an arrow deep infixed
> My panting side was charged, when I withdrew
> To seek a tranquil death in distant shades.
> *(The Task: The Garden)*

Yet this was not the worst of it. When he wrote these lines, he was comparatively serene, believing that though he had failed to make a career in society he had found a rescuer in Christ. In his worst state of mind he believed that he had been cast off by God Himself. In

Two portraits of Cowper by L. F. Abbott (left) and G. Romney (right). The more formal of the two is the less revealing in character; the one wearing a cap brings out the simplicity, kindliness and sensitivity of the man. Cowper characteristically feared and hated public formal occasions.

what has been called his one truly great poem, *The Castaway*, he compares his condition of pathological depression to that of a man fallen overboard in a storm—an incident he had read about in Anson's journal of his *Voyage Round the World* (1748). No help was possible: the seamen could do nothing but watch their comrade's death struggles in the waves. Cowper likewise believed that he was drowning in his despair; convinced of his rejection by God, he could hope for nothing from his friends, though he was conscious of their compassion and their longing to draw him back:

> No voice divine the storm allay'd
>   No light propitious shone;
> When, snatch'd from all effectual aid,
>   We perish'd, each alone;
> But I, beneath a rougher sea,
> And whelm'd in deeper gulfs than he.

The last two lines, in which he compares himself to the physically drowning man, are not hyperbolical, for Cowper was sure that his lot was eternal damnation. The pathos of the whole poem is enhanced by the contrast between the desperate personal matter and the formal, impersonal pattern of the stanzas and the diction. Even in his despair Cowper shared the eighteenth-century assumption that poetry was a public and a social art.

But it is compatible with the known character of Cowper's type of morbid delusion that he should not have been at all a morbid man; for many years he was even a happy one. His letters are famous for their grace, warmth and simplicity, and these seem to have been his predominant qualities in his personal relationships, as they are in much of his happier verse. It is in his poetry that he shows that side of the later eighteenth-century mind which contrasts with Johnson's. They shared an immense contempt for affectation and emotional flightiness, but whereas Johnson attacked them with the excoriating contempt of his reason, Cowper used, mostly, a gay and graceful satire which easily modulates into serious rhapsodies for those people, themes and scenes which evoked for him the most solemn and purest feelings. The people whom he loved best were those who were capable of responding genuinely and deeply to the themes and scenes, and these were especially religious and natural. In his poem *Conversation*, he begins by making witty fun of obsessive talkers, arrogant intellectuals, fashionable chatterers, and those who are so morbidly shy (through vanity, he diagnoses) that they can hardly converse at all. Then he comes to his main point: that serious and sensitive minds will naturally want to talk sincerely about the most serious matters, and that those who deride such conversation ought themselves to be the object of ridicule. He stigmatizes 'fashion, leader of a chatt'ring train', who ordains

> That he who dares, when she forbids, be grave,
> Shall stand proscrib'd, a madman or a knave,
> A close designer not to be believ'd,
> Or if excus'd that charge at least deceiv'd.

The serious mind, for Cowper, naturally resorted to religious subjects, or at least refused to allow these to be treated frivolously when they arose. But it was natural for a religious man of the eighteenth century to feel that love of the natural environment was, if not itself religious, at least closely related to religious feeling. Eighteenth-century scientists (known as 'natural philosophers') had a new curiosity about nature and were fascinated by the evidence of design and purpose in its phenomena. They had not yet propounded the evolutionary hypotheses (such as those of Lyell in geology and Darwin in biology) which in the nineteenth century came to seem in contradiction with traditional beliefs about a Divine Creator. On the contrary, for men like Cowper, nature was itself direct evidence of a Providence governing the world. He called attention to the religious feelings that Nature aroused in those willing to contemplate even a trivial natural scene:

> The love of Nature's works
> Is an ingredient in the compound, man,
> Infus'd at the creation of the kind.
> *(The Task: Winter Evening)*

The Task is the longest and best known of Cowper's works. Throughout, he extols the life of the man who seeks retirement and defends him against charges of idleness, uselessness and emptiness. Much of the moralizing is dated, but the poem lives by the quiet clarity and authenticity of the passages about natural scenery, not merely because they are separately fine 'pen pictures' but because cumulatively they show a convincing basis for Cowper's attacks on the abuses of society, of the innocent mind, and of the natural world. An example of such a passage is the following. The opening of the quotation is the end of an extended description of a quiet winter landscape:

> No noise is here, or none that hinders thought.
> The red-breast warbles still, but is content
> With slender notes, and more than half suppressed:
> Pleased with his solitude, and flitting light
> From spray to spray, where'er he rests he shakes
> From many a twig the pendent drops of ice,
> That tinkle in the withered leaves below.
> Stillness accompanied with sounds so soft,
> Charms more than silence. Meditation here

May think down hours to moments. Here the heart
May give a useful lesson to the head,
And learning wiser grow without his books.
(Winter Walk at Noon)

So Cowper proceeds to a disquisition on the distinction between Knowledge and Wisdom, and the various ways in which books can be a false guide even to Knowledge, much more to Wisdom. But

Lanes in which the primrose ere her time
Peeps through the moss that cloaths the hawthorn root
Deceive no student.

It is poetry of an intense, personal sensibility; reading it is often like experiencing an intimate conversation with a truthful but very private mind. One of Jane Austen's recurrent themes is the ways in which literature can shape, nourish and sometimes to some degree distort a character's attitudes to the world; a subtle example of this is that of the most 'Cowperesque' of her heroines, Fanny Price in *Mansfield Park*.

Fanny Price is separated from her own family at the age of nine because of its size and poverty; from then on she is brought up in the mansion of her rich uncle Sir Thomas Bertram. She is shy, retiring, diffident, and physically delicate, but she has strong, naïve, outgoing affections; her earliest and abiding love is for her brother William, but when she is separated from him, she develops an equally warm regard for her cousin Edmund, the only one of her rich relations who does not tease, bully, patronize, exploit or condescend to her. Because of her genuine humility and warmth of heart, she does not become embittered or sick, but she is driven upon her own resources, and it is not surprising to find her uttering this kind of reflection:

'Here's harmony!' said she, 'Here's repose! Here's what may leave all painting and all music behind, and what poetry can only attempt to describe. Here's what may tranquillize every care, and lift the heart to rapture! When I look out on such a night as this, I feel as if there could be neither wickedness nor sorrow in the world; and there certainly would be less of both if the sublimity of Nature were more attended to, and people were carried more out of themselves by contemplating such a scene.'

Readers have found this a little embarrassing; the speech is a little too shaped by rhetoric to be altogether spontaneous, and if one has been reading Cowper (a very popular poet at the time) it is difficult not to feel that Fanny is indeed being 'Cowperesque'. She tends to have Cowper in her mind: she quotes him twice in the novel, once to herself. Certainly Cowper would have agreed with the sentiment, as does Edmund:

> 'I like to hear your enthusiasm, Fanny . . . they are much to be pitied who have not been taught to feel in some degree as you do . . . They lose a great deal.'
> '*You* taught me to think and feel on the subject, cousin.'

Edmund suggests going out on to the lawn to look at the stars; Fanny gladly agrees, but at this moment the Crawfords and his sisters, 'fashion's chatt'ring train', begin singing a glee at the piano; Edmund drifts away to them and forgets.

In a letter to Cassandra in January 1813, Jane Austen, after some remarks about *Pride and Prejudice*, goes on: 'Now I will try and write of something else, & it shall be a complete change of subject—ordination.' She is usually taken to be referring to her next novel, *Mansfield Park*. But the remark has puzzled critics, because although Edmund is a candidate for ordination, and the novel contains, as we have seen, an amount of discussion about the clergy, their worldliness, and their proper relationship to society, it does not seem to have ordination as its subject. In the light of Cowper's life, work and religious feelings, however, perhaps we can see that nonetheless this is the case—provided we consider the theme in relation to Fanny and her influence on Edmund, and do not try to centre it on Edmund himself.

Edmund taught Fanny 'to think and feel' about nature and its influence on the spirit, and Cowper would be his most natural vehicle for teaching her—more natural than the early Wordsworth who was religiously less orthodox. Fanny takes naturally to the teaching because she resembles Cowper in her simplicity, unresentful sense of oppression, and warmth of affection. Edmund and his brother and sisters have been governed by the severe, high principles of their father, Sir Thomas, but Sir Thomas discovers by the end of the story that he has made a great error in failing to educate and call out his children's—and his own—feelings. The result is that they all, except Edmund, release their energies into shallow amusements and play with their emotions, with disastrous consequences. Their friends and the Crawfords do much to precipitate this confusion by their lively and heartless interventions: Sir Thomas's dull principles are no match for their lively wit. Edmund alone takes his father's principles to heart, and this makes him more serious in his feelings; all the same, he cannot escape the family ethos, and Mary Crawford very nearly traps him in her shallows. If Fanny saves him it is not by repeating back his lessons to her; teachers are gratified but rarely stimulated by that performance, and when Fanny engages in it, Edmund prefers Mary, who challenges and contradicts him. It is the spirit of Cowper which Fanny naturally possesses which eventually wins him. The paradox of the book is that isolated, weak, uncompetitive, vulnerable as she is, she is yet stronger than her antagonists because she alone has the true instinct for living: she alone lives by spontaneous affections. Cowper, a mental patient, unable to earn a living, unworldly to the point of helplessness, had that kind of strength; in consequence of it, he emerged, in spite of his despair, as the most respected poet and one of the leading influences on opinion of his time. He did not feel fit to become a clergyman, but Jane Austen is perhaps implying that his spirit ought to inspire a candidate for ordination.

I have tried to show that Jane Austen's work is thus suspended between the background influences of Johnson and Cowper, and to convey that the values of the former are represented most purely in the Knightley brothers, and those of the latter in Fanny Price. These characters have not on the whole been favourites with Jane Austen's readers, but this may be because their true principles of action and the bases of her morality have seldom been understood. Johnson's reason, Cowper's faith in feeling, complement each other like the masculine and feminine principles of her art. But they do so because neither writer denies or contradicts the other's premises. On the contrary these premises supplement each other, by a common basis of good faith in the concern of both writers for human need.

6 Literary Contemporaries: Isolation and Involvement

Johnson and Cowper embodied their own age for many of their contemporaries, as certain writers do again and again in history. Of the two Johnson was decidedly the greater, and counts for more today; Cowper is often seen as a mere forerunner—though this is both to misinterpret him and to do him injustice—of the romantic writers, and particularly of Wordsworth. He was not merely their predecessor, but a man, like Johnson, very much of his period—the period not yet shaken by the French Revolution and by the Napoleonic convulsion. They both believed in a fundamental permanence of the human condition, and saw change as evidence of superficial decay and degeneration. The romantics—especially Wordsworth and Coleridge in the eighteenth century when they were young—also believed in fundamental permanences, in qualities that made for survival of what is best in humanity, but they were more inclined to see change as regenerative; the fundamentals, for them, were thickly obscured and in need of visionary insight for their recovery. Johnson and Cowper saw them as self-evident to the normal faculties, and even accorded recognition by society, however superficially, as requisite to its own secure basis. When Johnson told Boswell to clear his *mind* of cant, when he and Cowper condemned affectation and declared that the basis of all excellence is truth, they were appealing to an ultimate criterion available to all who were not blinded by dishonesty and selfishness. When Wordsworth explained in his Preface to the *Lyrical Ballads* (1800) that his poems mainly treated 'humble and rustic life' because 'in that condition the passions of men were incorporated with the beautiful and permanent forms of nature', he was implying that urbanized men of all social levels were no longer in touch with the 'inherent and indestructible qualities of the human mind' within themselves.

All the same, it is, of course, true that in their common response to the natural environment, Cowper and Wordsworth were closer to each other than either was to Johnson. And since Cowper—according to her brother Henry—was Jane Austen's favourite poet, one accordingly expects some evidence that she was at least interested in Wordsworth's poetry. Perhaps indeed she was, but Henry does not say so, nor is Wordsworth's name mentioned anywhere in her writings. The contemporaries whom she admired among the poets were the conservative figures—Scott with his ballads and romances, and Crabbe with his eighteenth-century couplets.

She was not only—as far as the evidence goes—conservative in her poetic taste; she was also extraordinarily isolated from con-

58

temporary writers. Wordsworth, Coleridge, Southey, Scott, Byron, Lamb, Hazlitt, De Quincey, Shelley, Godwin, the Hunts—each knew at least some of the others, and if they did not meet personally they encountered each other in debates in the periodicals. Even Blake, the arch-outsider, in his youth had friends among the leading radical intellectuals such as Joseph Priestley and Tom Paine; even Crabbe, also a rather isolated figure, had his patrons in high society and sometimes met other writers. There is no evidence that Jane Austen met any of them. The one exception, a minor one, was Sir Samuel Egerton Brydges, a family connection on her mother's side, and the brother of her best friend, Anna Lefroy. He was a man who seems to have combined enormous social vanity with equivalent literary vanity—a mixture of Sir Walter Elliot in *Persuasion* and the heroines who caricature the cult of sensibility in *Love and Freindship*. Jane Austen does not seem to have thought much of him. One of her few references to him in her letters is on the subject of his novel, *Arthur Fitzalbini* (1798): 'My father is disappointed—I am not, for I expected nothing better. Never did any book carry more internal evidence of its author. Every sentiment is completely Egerton's' (vol. 1, p.32). Her personal isolation from the leading writers of her day, together with the conservatism of her literary tastes, have been taken to imply that study of her work can have little to do with contemporary literary and intellectual debates, and must chiefly concern her personal view of her social environment and her judgments of it as they were influenced by writers of her immediate past, such as Johnson and Cowper.

Until recently, this has been the usual opinion of her critics, both admirers and detractors. However, since 1970, a number of studies have taken a different attitude, arguing that on closer inspection she was not merely a bystander to contemporary events and currents of opinion, but a participant in them. The change has been stimulated by a new interest in the fiction of her contemporaries. On the whole, the fiction of the close of the eighteenth century has been largely ignored, regarded as distinguished by a few minor classics, such as Fanny Burney's *Evelina* (1778), William Godwin's *Caleb Williams* (1794), and Maria Edgeworth's *Castle Rackrent* (1800), and otherwise by works of chiefly historical interest, such as Henry Mackenzie's *The Man of Feeling* (1771) and Robert Bage's *Hermsprong* (1796). Conventional assumptions can often reduce the appeal of literary works below their merit: *Hermsprong* has been serialized on Radio 4, and this is not likely to happen to a work of no popular interest. It is still more important to recognize that a period which seems not to have produced much of importance in a particular form may not only be underestimated but may also have been very lively in the use of it ideologically. As long ago as 1932 J. M. S. Tompkins, in *The Popular Novel in England, 1770–1800*, showed how fruitful were the last thirty years of the eighteenth century in fiction; recently, in *Jane Austen and the War of Ideas*, Marilyn Butler has demonstrated its vigour in ideological contest. Whether Jane Austen can or should be read as taking sides in the political and social disputes of her time is a question to be considered later; first, it is at least useful to outline these as part of the climate in which she was working.

The eighteenth century has been commonly known as the 'Age of Reason', dominated as it was in its opening decades by Isaac Newton (1642–1727), one of the most influential of all European scientists. However, reason may induce scepticism, and scepticism can bite the tail of rationalism, stimulating a reaction against itself. One of the most influential thinkers to occasion a reversal of the dependence on reason was the philosopher David Hume (1711–76), whose scepticism encouraged the view that, however great the respect paid by human nature to reason, it was seldom guided by it. Human nature is motivated by its emotions, induced by the circumstances in which human beings find themselves in society, advantageous or otherwise. Such an attitude is ambiguous: it may encourage the belief that human beings seldom arrive at sound conclusions about their welfare, which is best left to those who can judge them disinterestedly; it may, on the contrary, nourish the belief that the cultivation of feeling is what really matters, and that most individuals are in some degree the victims of a society which, in its institutions governed by vested interests, is intrinsically unfeeling. The latter attitude stimulated the trend of 'sentimentalism', a natural fuel for the spirit of radical reform especially in imaginative literature.

English sentimentalism, imported to France, helped to stimulate the French Revolution, which broke out in 1789 (when Jane Austen was fourteen) and passed through terrifying crises until 1795. The Revolution hardened ideological differences in England, and an influential periodical, *The Anti-Jacobin*, founded in 1798, defined them by designating English radicals as 'Jacobins', thus aligning them with the extreme French Revolutionary party. However, although in France the soil for revolution had been prepared by sentimentalism, especially through the writings of Jean-Jacques Rousseau (1712–78), its influence in England was tamer and more mixed. It is manifest with most distinction in fiction in the novels of Laurence Sterne—*Tristram Shandy* (1767) and *A Sentimental Journey* (1768)—and with less distinction but much contemporary notoriety those of Henry Mackenzie in the seventies, but it had a more mixed response among the 'Jacobins', including, among writers of novels, William Godwin, Thomas Holcroft, and Robert Bage, who believed that social and political reform must derive from Reason. Thus, although sentimentalism had great public appeal, the play of reason and emotion tended to confuse the radical intellectuals, and there tended to be a corresponding confusion in religious circles. English Dissenters included some of the radical leaders, but among Anglicans the Evangelical movement, which sought to inspire congregations with an enthusiasm absent from the Anglican establishment, was conservative in its political and social influence. Thus, in England, sentimentalism—the cultivation of the emotions and of sensibility—did not influence public opinion all in one way; it could incite sympathy for others but it could also be egotistic and self-indulgent; it could excite desires for social change, but it could also compensate for social disadvantage so as to inhibit reform. On either side, however, it tended to disturb convention and inherited principles of behaviour, introducing discontinuities and instability into society.

The level of education had steadily risen among women through the century; they had steadily increased their proportion of the reading public, especially of fiction. Since literature was one of the few professions open to them, it is accordingly not surprising that women novelists were conspicuous in the years of Jane Austen's youth. Since public roles were still closed to them, most concentrated on the areas of their own social experience, and it was natural that, given the relative uncertainty of values in that era of threatening change, they should often choose as subject the comparatively educated young girl, able to use her faculties but much more imperilled by the risks of experiment than their brothers, and hence especially vulnerable both to the ignorance and prejudice of the older generation and to the recklessness and affectations of peers of either sex. The novels of Jane West—notably, *A Gossip's Story* (1796), a novel with resemblances to Jane Austen's *Sense and Sensibility*—criticize emotional impulsiveness when it becomes a substitute for principles of conduct. Fanny Burney's *Cecilia* and *Camilla* (1782 and 1796), and Maria Edgeworth's *Belinda* (1801) are all novels about young girls finding their identities in relation to their feelings and to society, implying a balance between reason and emotion, and discrimination between those in their environments who have achieved such a balance and the others who are dominated by selfishness and infatuation, or by prejudice and meaningless convention. Such novels are conservative inasmuch as they do not envisage material change in institutions or the class structure, but they are socially relevant inasmuch as they concern the values by which social relationships should be conducted.

That Jane Austen was influenced by such writers is evident not only from the character of her own work, but also from the mention of three of their novels in her unique passage of polemic, defending the novel as a literary form, in chapter 5 of *Northanger Abbey*. However, there is room for doubt whether it is merely the success of the novelists in their medium which has impressed her, or their ideological message, or whether, taken in its context, the passage has a subtler significance than mere eulogy of either:

Although our productions have afforded more extensive and un-affected pleasure than those of any other literary corporation in the world, no species of composition has been so decried ... 'I am no novel-reader—I seldom look into novels—Do not imagine that *I* often read novels—It is really very well for a novel.' Such is the common cant. 'And what are you reading, Miss—?' 'Oh! it is only a novel!' replies the young lady; while she lays down her book with affected indifference, or momentary shame. 'It is only *Cecilia*, or *Camilla*, or *Belinda*'; or, in short, only some work in which the greatest powers of the mind are displayed, in which the most thorough knowledge of human nature, the happiest delineation of its varieties, the liveliest effusion of wit and humour, are conveyed to the world in the best-chosen language.

One critic has described Jane Austen's language here as 'impassioned', but perhaps we should not take it entirely at face value. The passage occurs as a digression from the description of the immature heroine, Catherine Morland, meeting her superficial friend, Isabella Thorpe, to read novels. However, the novel the girls are reading is not by Fanny Burney or Maria Edgeworth, or a novelist resembling them; it is *The Mysteries of Udolpho* (1794) by Mrs Radcliffe, of the sensationalist, so-called 'gothic' school which they discuss enthusiastically in the next chapter:

'Have you gone on with *Udolpho*?'

'Yes, I have been reading it ever since I woke; and I am got to the black veil.'

'Are you indeed? How delightful! Oh! I would not tell you what is behind the black veil for the world! Are you not wild to know?'

'Oh! yes, quite; what can it be?—But do not tell me—I would not be told on any account. I know it must be a skeleton; I am sure it is Laurentina's skeleton. Oh! I am delighted with the book! I should like to spend my whole life reading it, I assure you; if it had not been to meet you, I would not have come away from it for all the world.'

'Dear creature! how much I am obliged to you; and when you have finished *Udolpho*, we will read the Italian together; and I have made out a list of ten or twelve more of the same kind for you.'

Northanger Abbey is of course a satire on the gothic genre, a sensationalist extreme of the sentimentalist trend, but one has to wonder whether this conversation in chapter 6 does not alter the effect of the passage in the previous chapter. Was it written partly with tongue in cheek? There can be no doubt that Jane Austen's advocacy of the novel as a literary vehicle is genuine, but her praise of the Burney and Edgeworth novels— 'work in which the greatest powers of the mind are displayed'—seems hyperbolical, and burlesqued by the girls' infatuation with Mrs Radcliffe a page or two later. It is true that Burney and Edgeworth have a literary merit which has kept them in print for nearly two centuries, but then so has Radcliffe. It is of course also true that their novels have resemblance to her own, and that both are opposed to the gothic sensationalism, and this strongly suggests an allegiance of values. But the tirade is so unlike Jane Austen's usual authorial voice, working as it does obliquely through irony, that a third explanation seems plausible: that the tirade, taken with the ensuing dialogue, is itself partly ironical. The irony is that whether or not readers profess to despise novels, fiction none the less has a strong influence in shaping opinion through the emotions, so that it is judged according to its emotional appeal and not by rational standards. We read what gives us enjoyment, and the enjoyment is strongly affected not by what we believe life to be, but by what we want it to be. If we have an ideology, we want fiction to confirm and encourage our beliefs, or if we find reality boring, we seek in fiction an alternative version. This is not to say that she believed the detractors of novels to be right, but that such detraction is hypocritical: the novel reader who apologizes for the occupation has in reality not discovered a proper case for its defence. Honest fiction will seek to convey life as it is, but it can never be a substitute for life itself which tends to be the real, unacknowledged reason for reading it. She admired Fanny Burney and Maria Edgeworth for their truthfulness, but she is indicating that even her own admiration can be treated sceptically: it may be that they too can mislead readers if they are accepted as life as it is and not as fictions, which are serious insofar as they are intended to correct illusions and not to substitute them by others.

If Jane Austen had an ideology, then for the appreciation of her work, it is less helpful to seek it in her politics or even in her probably strong religious faith, than in her attitude to the relationship of art to reality. All her novels convey as one of their themes the errors into which characters fall by their susceptibility to fiction. In three of them (*Northanger Abbey, Sense and Sensibility, and Mansfield Park*) it is literature itself which is the misleading influence. In *Northanger Abbey* Catherine Morland is so naïve as to suppose that her own life will turn into material for a gothic novel; in *Sense and Sensibility*, Marianne Dashwood believes that life should be lived in terms of the romantic emotions nourished by her reading, and that reasoning people cannot feel; in *Mansfield Park*, characters confuse their relationships by performing in a play which enables them to act out their secret desires without respect for their responsibilities. In *Persuasion*, a similar device is used, though only for a minor character—Captain Benwick, who transforms his grief for the death of his fiancée into a pleasure by indulging himself in mournful literature of sentiment, only to forget his sorrow very quickly when he discovers a new attachment. In the other two novels (*Pride and Prejudice* and *Emma*) the heroines are misled by two young men (Wickham and Churchill respectively) who act out parts with direct intention to deceive, and thereby sustain the illusions which the heroines wish to confirm. Implicit in her artistic ideology is the belief that we all incline to be our own novelists, creating the world in the image that best suits our weaknesses, so that we tend to draw from human relationships and from the literature we prefer whatever best nourishes our fictions of ourselves. The aim of her own novels, and the function of her constant irony, is both to show how such self-regarding fictions can be undermined, and to undermine any tendency in her own readers to misuse hers.

This does not mean that her personal aesthetics have no relevance to contemporary conflicts of ideas. Implicit in her viewpoint is the belief that ideology can itself be the basis for self-contrived illusions, whether through sentimentalism (like Henry Crawford's) that releases the character from responsibility, or through convention (like Sir Thomas Bertram's) that assumes feeling to be subordinate to material interests. Her conservatism is not complacent or anti-radical, but realistic. Her view of society is that it is to the individual what water is to the fish, which has to swim however foul the element, but she does not ignore its foulness when it is to her purpose to expose it. Her personal isolation from her leading contemporaries was no doubt partly accidental, due to her family circumstances, but it may partly have been self-chosen: it helped her to keep clear of the confusions of the ideological disputes. But personal isolation is not the same as obliviousness: she knew the work of the writers she never met and made use of them when it suited her. In particular, she cannot have been ignorant of the contemporary feminist controversies, which will be the subject of a later chapter. There is also no doubt that her reading of the novelists fascinated her with the novel as a form, and to understand this fascination it is important to remember that the form was comparatively new, the creation of the century in which she was born. Consequently we will next consider how the form had developed in ways that she must have studied, and the new shape she gave to it.

7 The Eighteenth-century Novel

The novel has always been a social form in two special senses: it has concerned itself more closely than any other literary form with social problems, manners, and organization; and (at least in England) it has been the product of one particular class—the middle class. Other narrative forms, of course, have had affinities with one social class rather than another: the medieval high romance belonged to the aristocracy; the ballad, to the folk. But these older forms did not necessarily express the values and the way of life of the classes that favoured them, although they tended to do so. The novel, in the eighteenth and nineteenth centuries, was more distinctly the outcome of middle-class values and outlook, not only in its characteristic content but in its characteristics as a composition. It is true that the middle class was so broad as to include widely various categories: Bunyan, who had intimate ties with village folk, perhaps marked its lower extreme, and Fielding, with his aristocratic relations, its upper one. Both contributed with distinction to the development of the novel form, for though *Pilgrim's Progress* (1678) can scarcely be called a novel, it has important novelistic qualities.

Between the two came distinctly middle-class writers such as Defoe and Richardson, rival progenitors of the true novel; Smollett, Sterne, and Fanny Burney. Jane Austen makes no reference to Bunyan or Smollett; it is difficult to believe that she was ignorant of the former and easier to believe that she never read the latter. The rest she knew, as well as many other forgotten and half forgotten writers, and works of fiction on the fringe of the form, such as Swift's *Gulliver's Travels*, Johnson's *Rasselas*, and Goldsmith's *Vicar of Wakefield*. She not only knew them; she learned from them, and shaped a perfect artistic coherence to which each contributed distinctive elements.

Any major literary form is a way of interpreting experience—one might say it is a 'shape of experience'—which grows up in a particular phase of civilization and survives that phase, if at all, much altered or with diminished vitality. It resembles a kind of plant life, which flourishes in a particular soil and climate, and usually derives nourishment from other forms which find the same environment congenial. In the eighteenth century the middle classes, partly because their very existence depended on an essentially practical outlook, partly because the Puritan ethic, which influenced them so strongly, suspected fiction as falsification of experience, encouraged forms of writing which were the outcome of daily living and its problems, or recorded the progress of mundane affairs. This was the century when modern journalism took shape, the first great biography (Boswell's of Johnson) was written, and private correspondence was cultivated as an art. It is no accident that Defoe not only has claims to be our first eminent novelist but was our first eminent journalist, and that Richardson's novels are composed of letters exchanged between the characters. It is relevant that Fielding, before he became a novelist, was a dramatist and theatre manager: the eighteenth-century comedies of sentiment and manners, undistinguished as most of them were, also had lessons to teach the novelist, in setting a scene and conveying its meaning through dialogue.

Daniel Defoe, 1660–1731

The journalist offers fact, or—what is equally significant for the novelist—the illusion of fact. He and the novelist in this respect resemble the historian: they have the same kind of respect for truth. (Here one is reminded of yet another aspect of the eighteenth century of relevance to the novelist, that it was the first age of great British historians, at least of the modern kind.) Compare the following openings, the first of *Robinson Crusoe* and the second of Jane Austen's novel, *Emma*:

I was born in the year 1632, in the city of York, of a good family, though not of that country, my father being a foreigner of Bremen, named Kreutznaer, who settled first at Hull. He got a good estate by merchandise, and leaving off his trade, lived afterwards at York; from whence he had married my mother, whose relations were named Robinson, a very good family in that country, and after whom I was so called, that is to say, Robinson Kreutsnaer; but, by the usual corruption of words in England, we are now called, nay, we call ourselves, and write our name, Crusoe; and so my companions always called me.

I had two elder brothers, one of whom was lieutenant-colonel to an English regiment of foot in Flanders, formerly commanded by the famous Colonel Lockhart, and was killed at the battle near Dunkirk against the Spaniards. What became of my second brother, I never knew, any more than my father and mother did know what was become of me.

Emma Woodhouse, handsome, clever, and rich, with a comfortable home and happy disposition, seemed to unite some of the blessings of existence; and had lived nearly twenty-one years in the world with very little to distress or vex her.

She was the youngest of the two daughters of a most affectionate, indulgent father, and had, in consequence of her sister's marriage, been mistress of the house from a very early period. Her mother had died too long ago for her to have more than an indistinct remembrance of her caresses, and her place had been supplied by an excellent woman as governess, who had fallen little short of a mother in affection.

Sixteen years had Miss Taylor been in Mr Woodhouse's family, less as a governess than a friend, very fond of both daughters, but particularly of Emma. Between *them* it was more the intimacy of sisters. Even before Miss Taylor had ceased to hold the nominal office of governess, the mildness of her temper had hardly allowed her to impose any restraint; and the shadow of authority being now long passed away, they had been living together as friend and friend very mutually attached, and Emma doing just what she liked; highly esteeming Miss Taylor's judgement, but directed chiefly by her own.

Each novelist communicates the factual circumstances of the character to whom the reader is being introduced. But each uses a strategy in doing so: Defoe and Jane Austen not merely tell the reader what he needs to know, but unobtrusively guide his attention towards certain inferences. We learn that Crusoe's father was a prosperous merchant; it prepares us for Crusoe's capacity to make and use wealth—to turn himself into a 'man of substance' in almost any circumstances in which he finds himself. But we also learn that the father had been a foreigner, that one brother had mysteriously disappeared and the other had been killed in a battle. The father had been enterprising enough to seek his prosperity in a foreign country, therefore, and the sons had been restless and adventurous. Put the two qualities—the concern for wealth and the love of adventure—together, and you have Crusoe's story epitomized; even his name is an epitome, Robinson suggesting the practical, businesslike sobriety which is one side of his character, and Crusoe reflecting the wanderer, in love with the unknown. Jane Austen shows us a girl to whom life has dealt an exceptionally favourable hand of cards, but at the same time indicates the risks of such good fortune: Emma is used to having her own way without having learned anything about the disagreeable aspects of authority or responsibility, or even about the difficult sides of ordinary human relationship. Her opening offers scope for more and more delicate inferences than Defoe's—consider the irony of her last sentence—but they are engaged in essentially the same operation.

Defoe contrives his stories so that they always read plausibly as accounts of fact, but he is much less interested in states of mind, except in so far as his characters undergo the great primary emotions, such as anger, terror, despair, hope, relief and exultation. His personal relationships are on the whole utilitarian, even with wives; Robinson values Man Friday as a devotedly reliable servant, and his warmest expression of feeling is towards a Portuguese landowner who manages Robinson's South American estates for him conscientiously during his long absence on the island.

To express a complex and conflicting emotion is not perhaps a function one attributes to journalists; it is, on the other hand, a familiar characteristic of the private letter-writer that he at least attempts to do just this. As letter-writers, we display our personalities to our friends, we give ourselves away—sometimes most when we are defending ourselves—and we seek counsel and sympathy. It follows that the epistolary novelist, who composes his novels entirely of letters, gives himself the opportunity of imagining one temperament after another, identifying with each as each seeks to express his or her own conflicts, fears, and passions. Of course the method has its own strong disadvantages, especially in the risk of improbability: in real life, even in the eighteenth century, private letters have seldom been the vehicle of a long, fully coherent narrative, or even could be. Yet the method was plausible in the eighteenth century, and its advantages strong, and few if any epistolary novelists have understood its advantages so well as its first user, Samuel Richardson. This may have been because, as we shall see, he cultivated the letter as an art before, late in life, he cultivated the hitherto little explored art of the novel.

Samuel Richardson, 1689–1761

There are several evident reasons why the art of writing letters should have flourished in the eighteenth century. Communications were good enough to give reasonable certainty to their arrival, but not so good that friends and relatives could see each other often and easily. More important still, education was spreading fairly rapidly, though very unevenly, and many more people could write with facility than ever before. There was also a taste for reading among many who had received little regular education; Richardson himself describes how he improved his mind in the few hours allowed to him as a printer's apprentice by a very hard master. By middle age he was well known among printers and booksellers (the publishers of the day) as a useful man with the pen, and in 1739 he was asked to compile a volume of model letters for the use of people who lacked the education to take to letter-writing easily. From this he got the idea of writing a morally instructive story, and so *Pamela* originated.

Portrait of Richardson by J. Highmore. The portrait shows the rather naïve, self-conscious pomposity and complacency of the professional moralizer who could yet rise to be a great novelist when he released the artist within himself.

Samuel Richardson, Author of Clarissa

He did not think of it as a work of art, but as a work of moral didactics; yet he found himself faced with the task of putting himself in the mind of a young, beautiful and communicative servant girl, isolated from her parents to whom she writes, and in the power of her employer, a country gentleman called throughout 'Mr B.', who falls in love with her and tries every device he can to seduce her before he at last makes up his mind to marry her. He secures that she is put in the charge of a lascivious and unscrupulous older servant, Mrs Jewkes, who is entirely at his disposal to serve his object. But Pamela is also attracted to Mr B.; she only refuses to become a 'thing' to serve his lusts. When Mrs Jewkes is out on a visit, Pamela conceives it her duty to run away, but cannot bring herself to achieve her purpose. She is frightened of being seen; she is frightened of what she thinks to be a bull in a neighbouring field; partly she does not want to escape at all.

> Well, here I am, come back again! frightened, like a fool, out of all my purposes! O how terrible every thing appears to me! I had got twice as far again, as I was before, out of the back-door: and I looked and saw the bull, as I thought, between me and the door; and another bull coming towards me the other way: Well, thought I, here is double witchcraft, to be sure! Here is the spirit of my master in one bull, and Mrs Jewkes's in the other. And now I am gone, to be sure! O help! cried I, like a fool, and ran back to the door, as swift as if I flew. When I had got the door in my hand, I ventured to look back, to see if these supposed bulls were coming; and I saw they were only two poor cows, a grazing in distant places, that my fears had made all this rout about. But as every thing is so frightful to me, I find I am not fit to think of my escape: for I shall be as much frightened at the first strange man that I meet with: and I am persuaded, that fear brings one into more dangers, than the caution, that goes along with it, delivers one from.
>
> I then locked the door, and put the key in my pocket, and was in a sad quandary; but I was soon determined; for the maid Nan came in sight, and asked, if any thing was the matter, that I was so often up and down stairs? God forgive me, (but I had a sad lie at my tongue's end,) said I; Though Mrs Jewkes is sometimes a little hard upon me, yet I know not where I am without her: I go up, and I come down to walk in the garden; and, not having her, know scarcely what to do with myself. Ay, said the ideot, she is main good company, madam, no wonder you miss her.

A bull is a familiar symbol of sexual aggression. Mr B. and Mrs Jewkes are allied in a pincer-movement of sexual design upon her; it is appropriate that she should identify them with the two 'bulls' advancing upon her from different directions. Pamela projects her inward fears into images of immediate physical danger, but her real state of mind is more complicated than that. She does not want to be raped—indeed she is determined not to be—but she does desire Mr B., as he desires her. Her physical ditherings, her optical delusions, cannot be explained to Nan, or even fully explained to herself, but their secret can be 'given away' by her recounting of them. Perhaps even her irritated abuse of Nan as an 'ideot' for calling Mrs Jewkes 'main good company' is a give-away: perhaps Mrs Jewkes is not merely Mr B.'s ally against Pamela, but also the ally of that part of Pamela that desires Mr B. against the part of her that resists him, and Pamela, of course, would be trying not to admit the fact, even to herself. It is often difficult to know how much Richardson the moral instructor knew what Richardson the artist was up to; it is certain that the artist often went further than the teacher intended.

Jane Austen did not suffer Richardson's division of purpose; she was all artist. In the following passage from *Mansfield Park*, Fanny Price is watching Edmund Bertram giving Mary Crawford a riding lesson, when he was supposed to be giving herself one:

> The houses, though scarcely half a mile apart, were not within sight of each other; but by walking fifty yards from the hall door she could look down the park, and command a view of the Parsonage and all its demesnes, gently rising beyond the village road; and in Dr Grant's meadow she immediately saw the group—Edmund and Miss Crawford both on horseback, riding side by side, Dr and Mrs Grant, and Mr Crawford, with two or three grooms, standing about and looking on. A happy party it appeared to her—all interested in one object—cheerful beyond a doubt, for the sound of merriment ascended even to her. It was a sound which did not make *her* cheerful; she wondered that Edmund should forget her, and felt a pang. She could not turn her eyes from the meadow, she could not help watching all that passed. At first Miss Crawford and her companion made the circuit of the field, which was not small, at a foot's pace; then, at *her* apparent suggestion, they rose into a canter; and to Fanny's timid nature it was most astonishing to see how well she sat. After a few minutes, they stopped entirely, Edmund was close to her, he was speaking to her, he was evidently directing her management of the bridle, he had hold of her hand; she saw it, or the imagination supplied what the eye could not reach. She must not wonder at all this; what could be more natural than that Edmund should be making himself useful, and proving his good-nature by any one? She could not but think, indeed, that Mr Crawford might as well have saved him the trouble; that it would have been particularly proper and becoming in a brother to have done it himself; but Mr Crawford, with all his boasted good-nature, and all his coachmanship, probably knew nothing of the matter, and had no active kindness in comparison

of Edmund. She began to think it rather hard upon the mare to have such double duty; if she were forgotten, the poor mare should be remembered.

Fanny is a poor relation, a child of charity, practically a servant like Pamela, though nominally on terms of equality with her cousins. Her state of mind is much less obscure than Pamela's, and her situation is at the other extreme inasmuch as she is very far from the danger of rape; she is only in danger of total neglect. Neglect of Fanny's sort may, of course, be as painful as rape, and it is much commoner. But it is not—though Cinderella is an exception and Fanny is a real-life Cinderella—usually 'a good story'; it does not make drama. Yet the scene *is*, of course, dramatic for Fanny, and Jane Austen makes it dramatic for us by making us see it with a mixture of detachment and involvement resembling, and yet differing from, Fanny's own detachment and involvement. She is detached physically because she is watching from a distance, and we see with her eyes— minutely but clearly; but she is involved because what she sees agitates her, and her agitation is conveyed to us through the slightly breathless syntax: 'they stopped . . . Edmund was close . . . he was speaking . . . he was evidently directing . . . he had hold of her hand . . . she saw it . . .' But she is also detached in a more painful and psychological sense, in that she knows that she has no right to the agitation she feels ('she must not wonder'). Her Aunt Norris would consider it the last impertinence for her to fall in love with Edmund, and since she is in love with him, and her mildness and humility has caused her to accept her Aunt Norris's version of her lot, she must conceal the state of her feelings even from herself. She does not wish, and certainly has no right, to blame Edmund; she has no reason to blame Mary, although in addition to every social right to his possession she has the unfair advantage of being able to sit a horse gracefully; she has very weak grounds for complaint against Mary's brother. So, since she must have some object on which to project her painful resentment, she identifies herself with the mare—or rather, does not precisely do this, because the mare, unlike herself, she knows to have acknowledged rights.

As we watch the process of her innocent casuistry, *we* are detached from the scene, but in a different psychological sense from Fanny; she is in the shadow of tragedy, but we are in the light of comedy. Fanny is telling herself a lie about which the author makes no comment, but she has enabled us to know the truth and why Fanny is evading it. It is the strategy of irony, a strategy constantly used by Jane Austen, with varying degrees of plainness or indirection, light-heartedness or intensity. She can use it with this delicacy, or with the blatancy of the opening sentence of *Pride and Prejudice*: 'It is a truth universally acknowledged, that a single man in possession of a good fortune must be in want of a wife.' In regard to Fanny it is used gently and forgivingly; in regard to Emma Woodhouse, it is used almost ferociously, and yet with such subtlety that many readers miss it altogether. It is on the whole a dramatic strategy, because it is based on a tension between what is real and what a character invents as reality; sometimes the invention is harmless (as in Fanny's case) or merely ridiculous; sometimes it is ominous with implications of tragedy for the liar, a tragedy which Emma narrowly escapes.

The weakness of Samuel Richardson for modern readers is what he would probably have been happy to confirm as his strength: the moralist in him too often took precedence of the artist. This is most evident in the last of his three novels—*Sir Charles Grandison* (1754), the portrayal of an ideal man, written apparently to balance that of the ideal woman in his two earlier novels, *Pamela* (1741) and *Clarissa Harlowe* (1748). It is mentioned in chapter 6 of *Northanger Abbey*, during the conversation about novels between Isabella Thorpe and Catherine Morland:

'... I suppose Mrs. Morland objects to novels.'

'No, she does not. She very often reads *Sir Charles Grandison* herself; but new books do not fall in our way.'

'*Sir Charles Grandison!* That is an amazing horrid book, is it not?—I remember Miss Andrews could not get through the first volume.'

'It is not like *Udolpho* at all; but yet I think it is very entertaining.'

'Do you indeed!—you surprise me; I thought it had not been readable ...'

Condemnation by Isabella is sure to be implicit recommendation by Jane Austen, and family tradition maintained that this novel was her favourite of the three. The preference has been indirectly confirmed by the discovery in 1977 that a play based on the novel and formerly thought to be by a niece is in fact Jane Austen's work. It is the slightest of sketches probably written for family entertainment, but although its tone is not as serious as Richardson's, it is evidently not intended as a burlesque but rather as a tribute. For once, modern readers may be inclined to side with Isabella's puzzlement against Jane Austen's judgment, but before we do so we should recall that George Eliot shared Jane Austen's enthusiasm for *Sir Charles Grandison*. An explanation may be the paradoxical one that because for once Richardson is idealizing a man and not a woman, the leading female characters have the licence of more natural vitality than do the heroines of the other two novels, with their burden of ideal exemplification.

Jonathan Swift, 1667–1745

Eighteenth-century writers especially cultivated irony; it is a form of expression which suited the strengths of the eighteenth-century mind, since it depends on a balance between a tough scepticism about human nature in its capacity to deceive itself, and a robust faith in the capacity of human reason to arrive at true judgments, given good sense, good will, and adequate self-knowledge. It is not much evident in Richardson; he was of Puritan descent, and the Puritans (except Bunyan) seem rather to have distrusted irony, perhaps because it was used so much against them. But it is conspicuous in Swift and Fielding. Swift used irony extensively to expose the contrast between a man's idea of himself as a social being, and his appearance to a mind which chooses to ignore his social pretensions; Fielding, to expose the contrast between the way society behaves and the way it professes to behave, between sham morality and true morality.

In *Gulliver's Travels*, Swift uses Gulliver not merely as the narrator of his tale but as the target of much of his satire. Gulliver is a kind of pattern of the middle-class English gentleman, complacent about the values of his society, proud of his education, breeding and manners. He takes everything at the face value which his assumptions about his civilization provide for him, but Swift so manages his predicaments as to expose the painful thinness of his valuations. We see him, for instance, strutting about the Brobdingnagian farmer's dining table, forty feet from the ground. To himself, he is still the English gentleman, parading before rustics in the pride of his superior refinement, while Swift shows plainly that they see him as something comparable to a performing mouse.

> Then the master made me a sign to come to his trencher side; but as I walked on the table . . . I happened to stumble against a crust, and fell flat on my face, but received no hurt. I got up immediately, and observing the good people to be in much concern, I took my hat (which I held under my arm out of good manners) and waving it over my head, made three huzzas, to show I had got no mischief by my fall. But advancing forward toward my master . . . his youngest son who sat next him, an arch boy of about ten years old, took me up by the legs, and held me so high in the air, that I trembled every limb; but his father snatched me from him, and at the same time gave him such a box on the ear, as would have felled a European troop of horse to the earth, ordering him to be taken from the table. But being afraid the boy might owe me a spite, and well remembering how mischievous all children among us naturally are to sparrows, rabbits, young kittens, and puppy dogs, I fell on my knees, and pointing to the boy, made my master to understand, as well as I could, that I desired his son might be pardoned. The father complied, and the lad took his seat again; whereupon I went to him and kissed his hand, which my master took, and made him stroke me gently with it.

Brobdingnag is in all respects like England except in its scale of dimensions. A Brobdingnagian Gulliver would kiss no one's hand but that of a fine lady; he would address a farmer as 'my man' instead of referring to him as 'my master', and might toss a penny to the 'arch' farmer's lad. The actual Gulliver knows when to be diplomatic, but his basic faith in his social status remains unshaken. Yet what becomes of our social valuations and fine breeding, Swift seems to be asking, if they can be shown to be so dependent on something so extraneous to value as mere size? And what connection need exist between our own estimate of our importance and the estimate of an observer who happens to be unimpressed by the evidence? Only at the end of his Travels, when Gulliver finds himself reverentially kissing the hoof of a horse, is his faith in the valuations of his own kind seriously shaken.

It is this kind of Swiftian irony that Jane Austen uses in such a passage as the following, from *Sense and Sensibility*:

On ascending the stairs, the Miss Dashwoods found so many people before them in the room, that there was not a person to attend to their orders . . . All that could be done was to sit down at that end of the counter which seemed to promise quickest succession; one gentleman only was standing there, and it is probable that Elinor was not without hope of exciting his politeness to a quicker despatch. But the correctness of his eye, and the delicacy of his taste, proved to be beyond his politeness. He was giving orders for a toothpick-case for himself; and till its size, shape, and ornaments were determined . . . he had no leisure to bestow any attention on the two ladies than what was comprised in three or four very broad stares; a kind of notice which seemed to imprint on Elinor the remembrance of a person and face of strong, natural, sterling insignificance, though adorned in the first style of fashion.

Marianne was spared from the troublesome feelings of contempt and resentment, on this impertinent examination of their features and on the puppyism of his manner in deciding on all the different horrors of the different toothpick-cases presented to his inspection, by remaining unconscious of it all; for she was as well able to collect her thoughts within herself, and be as ignorant of what was passing around her, in Mr Gray's shop, as in her own bedroom.

At last the affair was decided. The ivory, the gold, and the pearls, all received their appointment; and the gentleman having named the last day on which his existence could be continued without the possession of the toothpick-case, drew on his gloves with leisurely care, and bestowing another glance on the Miss Dashwoods, but such a one as seemed to rather demand than express admiration, walked off with a happy air of real conceit and affected indifference.

On the surface, this is too explicit for irony, which operates by stimulating the reader's inferences, whereas Elinor's contempt is made very clear. The real irony lies deeper than her feeling. Robert Ferrars (as the gentleman turns out to be) is so sure of his importance and of the deep and favourable impression he must make on two pretty young women, whereas one is thoroughly despising him and the other does not notice him at all. Jane Austen is fatalistic about this sort of character; he will remain in his self-complacence all his life, because he is impervious to criticism from anyone except such as he supposes his superiors in his style of fashion—in other words, in his own compound of arrogance and triviality. Swift similarly considered that whole classes of people were incapable of making human judgments except by their own trivial standards of social appearance and deportment, and he grimly concluded that this was just as well for them.

Henry Fielding, 1707–54

'I describe not men, but manners; not an individual, but a species', wrote Fielding in *Joseph Andrews*, thereby showing that he was a different sort of novelist from Richardson (and Jane Austen) and less of a novelist than they were, though this does not mean that he was a lesser writer. They also were interested in manners and species, but for them the main concern was the states of mind generated in individuals by the surrounding climate of manners, and by the generality of the human species. However, Fielding's concern with generalities enabled him to see his society panoramically beyond any other novelist of his century, and at his best he achieved a broad social satire which epitomizes some social attitudes with the permanence of a profound fable.

An example is the stage coach episode in *Joseph Andrews*. Joseph has just been beaten up by robbers, deprived of all his clothes, and left to perish by the wayside. A stage coach drives up, but although Joseph's very life is all too plainly at stake, unexpected obstacles delay his admission. One of the passengers is a lawyer who fears the legal consequences of leaving Joseph to perish, but a lady passenger declares that 'she had rather stay in that place for all eternity, than ride with a naked man'. An elderly gentleman takes the side of the lawyer, but for the different reason that he looks forward to making fun of the lady's embarrassment; however, the coachman insists that someone must pay Joseph's fare, and this both gentlemen refuse. The lawyer overcomes the coachman's objection by pointing out his legal obligations, but then a new difficulty arises: Joseph, who is the brother of Richardson's chaste Pamela, is himself so overcome by the lady's ostentatious horror at his nakedness that he himself refuses miserable as he was, to enter, unless he was furnished with sufficient covering to prevent giving the least offence to decency: so perfectly modest was this young man; such mighty effects had the spotless examples of the amiable Pamela, and the excellent sermons of Mr Adams, wrought upon him.

Though there were several great-coats about the coach, it was not easy to get over this difficulty which Joseph had started. The two gentlemen complained that they were cold, and could not spare a rag; the man of wit saying, with a laugh, that charity began at home; and the coachman, who had two great-coats spread under him, refused to lend either, lest they should be made bloody: the lady's footman desired to be excused for the same reason, which the lady herself, notwithstanding her abhorrence of a naked man, approved: and it is more than probable that Joseph, who obstinately adhered to his modest resolution, must have perished, unless the postilion (a lad who has been since transported for robbing a hen-roost) had voluntarily stripped off a great-coat, his only garment; at the same time swearing a great oath, for which he was rebuked by the passengers, that he would rather ride in his shirt all his life, than suffer a fellow-creature to lie in so miserable a condition.

Fielding is writing about morality. For the lady, a moral principle is what preserves her public decorum; for all the passengers, it is what is consistent with their comfort and the preservation of their property; for the coachman, it is sticking to the regulations of his employment. Only for the postilion, who probably does not entertain the concept at all, does morality have anything to do with the care of a fellow-creature, and he is rebuked for the 'immorality' of his oath and, in a parenthesis, doomed to a most exorbitant penalty for a most trivial offence. Morality, Fielding is saying, comes from the heart or not at all: the social conventions, the regulations, the legal system, private convenience, are all no doubt necessary in their proper place, but it is not for them to take the place of truly human morality even if they may sometimes happen to coincide with it.

Jane Austen does not deal in this kind of episode, which epitomizes timeless social illusions and deceits. Yet she does resemble Fielding in her frequent implications that values which receive social acceptance are often irrelevant or absurd when referred to true human needs and deserts. An obvious target for her comment of this kind is Sir Walter Elliot in *Persuasion*, 'who, for his own amusement, never took up any book but the Baronetage'. He is idle, useless and stupid, but he is sure that his fine appearance, his deportment and his rank offer the only respectable criteria for a fine society. The novel was written at the end of the Napoleonic War, when the navy had saved the country from conquest, and very likely saved Sir Walter's own

estate and person, but he despises sailors and objects to their profession:

> 'Yes; it is in two points offensive to me; I have two strong objections to it. First, as being the means of bringing persons of obscure birth into undue distinction, and raising men to honours which their fathers and grandfathers never dreamt of; and, secondly, as it cuts up a man's youth and vigour most horribly; a sailor grows old sooner than any other man. I have observed it all my life. A man is in greater danger in the navy of being insulted by the rise of one whose father his father might have disdained to speak to, and of becoming prematurely an object of disgust himself, than in any other line.'

His toady, Mrs Clay, is only too ready to corroborate his opinion; though she makes a show of deprecation:

> 'Nay, Sir Walter, . . . this is being severe indeed. Have a little mercy on the poor men. We are not all born to be handsome. The sea is no beautifier, certainly; sailors do grow old betimes; I have often observed it; they soon lose the look of youth. But then, is not it the same with many other professions, perhaps most others? Soldiers, in active service, are not at all better off; and even in the quieter professions, there is a toil and a labour of the mind, if not of the body, which seldom leaves a man's looks to the natural effect of time. The lawyer plods, quite care-worn: the physician is up at all hours, and travelling in all weather; and even the clergyman—' she stopped a moment to consider what might do for the clergyman—'and even the clergyman, you know, is obliged to go into infected rooms, and expose his health and looks to all the injury of a poisonous atmosphere. In fact, as I have long been convinced, though every profession is necessary and honourable in its turn, it is only the lot of those who are not obliged to follow any, who can live in a regular way, in the country, choosing their own hours, following their own pursuits, and living on their own property, without the torment of trying for more; it is only *their* lot, I say, to hold the blessing of health and a good appearance to the utmost: I know no other set of men but what lose something of their personableness when they cease to be quite young.'

So Sir Walter is confirmed in his faith—not that it needs any confirmation—that the emptiness of his life is not only compatible with

*Henry Fielding from an original by William Hogarth, a close and
influential friend. The portrait shows him before he began writing novels,
when he was celebrated in the comic theatre.*

but even the indispensable condition for the excellence of the qualities which he is proud to represent.

Fielding was a man of the theatre before he became a novelist, and one of his contributions to the art of the novel was his extensive use of animated and dramatic dialogue, though often, like Defoe and Richardson, he used a reported form, as in the extract we have quoted. But Fielding's dialogue generally lacks subtlety: it is good for representing his broad species of humanity, but it seldom reveals differentiation within the species, in the way that speech in real life betrays the finer idiosyncrasies of classes, types and individuals. Between Fielding and Jane Austen came another novelist from whom she must have learnt much about this more subtle and more dramatic use of dialogue. This was Fanny Burney.

Fanny Burney, 1752–1840

Fanny Burney does not retain the high status of the other writers in this section. She was without the insight of Richardson, without the breadth and sanity of Fielding; she did not equal Defoe in his extraordinary capacity for creating the illusion of a world of solid objects. She wrote four novels: *Evelina* (1778), *Cecilia* (1782), *Camilla* (1796), and *The Wanderer* (1814). Of these, the first remains a minor classic, the second and third tend to be left to students, and the last is forgotten. Her heroines are rather too beautiful, good and clever, and her heroes have hardly any flesh and blood at all; brought together, they talk in a high-flown diction never used by man or woman. Yet her novels have life, and part of this life comes from her acute ear for the spoken word, when it is not being spoken by a hero or a heroine, or at least when they are not speaking to each other. Her heroines frequently find themselves in very mixed society, giving scope for the clash of class idiom. Thus Cecilia finds herself in the pleasure gardens at Vauxhall, in the box of a man of fashion and in the company of a rake and two London tradesmen not at all used to the affectations of smart society:

> In a few minutes Captain Aresby, who was passing by the box, stopt to make his compliments to Mrs Harrel and Cecilia.
>
> 'What a concourse!' he cried, casting up his eyes with an expression of half-dying fatigue, 'are you not *accablé?* for my part I hardly respire. I have hardly ever had the honour of being so *obsédé* before.'
>
> 'We can make very good room, sir,' said Morrice, 'if you choose to come in.'
>
> 'Yes,' said Mr Simkins, obsequiously standing up, 'I am sure the gentleman will be very welcome to take my place, for I did not mean for to sit down, only just to look agreeable.'

Portrait of Fanny Burney by her cousin E. F. Burney after she had married her French husband and become Madame D'Arblay. In spite of the dressy hat and costume, the face retains the girlish unselfconsciousness which produced the revealing letters and Evelina.

'By no means, sir,' answered the Captain: 'I shall be quite *au désespoir* if I derange anybody.'

'Sir,' said Mr Hobson, 'I don't offer you my place, because I take it for granted if you had a mind to come in, you would not stand upon ceremony; for what I say is, let every man speak his mind, and then we shall all know how to conduct ourselves!'

The Captain, after looking at him with a surprise not wholly unmixt with horror, turned from him without making any answer, and said to Cecilia, 'And how long, ma'am, have you tried this petrifying place?'

'An hour,—two hours, I believe,' she answered.

'Really? and nobody here! *assez de monde*, but nobody here! a blank *partout!*'

'Sir,' said Mr Simkins, getting out of the box that he might bow with more facility, 'I humbly crave pardon for the liberty, but, if I understood right, you said something of a blank? pray, sir, if I may be so free, has there been anything of the nature of a lottery, or a raffle, in the garden? or the like of that?'

'Sir!' said the Captain, regarding him from head to foot, 'I am quite *assomé* that I cannot comprehend your allusion.'

'Sir, I ask pardon,' said the man, bowing still lower, 'I only thought if in case it should not be above half a crown, or such a matter as that, I might perhaps stretch a point once in a way.'

The Captain, more and more amazed, stared at him again, but not thinking it necessary to take any further notice of him, he enquired of Cecilia if she meant to stay late.

'I hope not,' she replied, 'I have already stayed later than I wished to do.'

'Really!' said he, with an unmeaning smile: 'Well, that is as horrid a thing as I have the *malheur* to know. For my part, I make it a principle not to stay long in these semi-barbarous places, for after a certain time they bore me to that degree I am quite *abîmé*. I shall, however, do *mon possible* to have the honour of seeing you again.'

And then, with a smile of yet greater insipidity, he protested he was *reduced to despair* in leaving her, and walked on.

'Pray, ma'am, if I may be so bold,' said Mr Hobson, 'what countryman may that gentleman be?'

'An Englishman, I suppose, sir,' said Cecilia.

'An Englishman, ma'am!' said Mr Hobson, 'why I could not understand one word in ten that came out of his mouth.'

If the Fielding passage was about morals, this one is about manners. Aresby's fashionable extravagance and Simkins's vulgar obsequiousness are both patently insincere; both are strategies, the one to gain a cheap prestige, and the other to gain whatever he can by deceit.

But Hobson's aggressive bluffness, as a longer extract would show, is equally an affectation: a strategy to gain what he can by bullying. Cecilia, who is at her best in this kind of mixed circle, is reduced to a kind of painful colourlessness; it is not only Aresby but all of them who are talking a 'foreign' language not meant to be understood, so that her own voice, which *is* meant to be understood, and her manners, which attempt sincerity, are muffled and baffled.

Jane Austen contrasts with Fanny Burney as she does with Fielding, inasmuch as she does not deal with such broad social categories, but her discriminations are not only finer, but deeper. The following example is a conversation from *Emma* (Chapter 34), provoked by a visit by Jane Fairfax to the post office for a letter—from her lover, though no one knows this. Jane is gifted but penniless and lonely, doomed to a lifetime as a governess if the wayward Frank Churchill does not play true. John Knightley (Mr Knightley's brother) begins the conversation with her; he is the straightforward businessman, devoted to his family. Mr Woodhouse, Emma's father, is an old-fashioned hypochondriac, and Mrs Elton, the affected vicar's wife, has chosen to take Jane under her 'protection'.

'. . . The post-office has a great charm at one period of our lives. When you have lived to my age, you will begin to think letters are never worth going through the rain for.'

There was a little blush, and then this answer, 'I must not hope to be ever situated as you are, in the midst of every dearest connexion, and therefore I cannot expect that simply growing older would make me indifferent about letters.'

'Indifferent! Oh! no—I never conceived you could become indifferent. Letters are no matters of indifference; they are generally a very positive curse.'

'You are speaking of letters of business; mine are letters of friendship.'

'I have often thought them the worse of the two,' replied he coolly. 'Business, you know, may bring money, but friendship hardly ever does.'

'Ah! you are not serious now. I know Mr John Knightley too well—I am very sure he understands the value of friendship as well as anybody. I can easily believe that letters are very little to you, much less than to me; but it is not your being ten years older than myself which makes the difference, it is not age, but situation. You have everybody dearest to you always at hand—I, probably, never shall again; and therefore, till I have outlived all my affections, a post-office, I think, must always have power to draw me out, in worse weather than to-day.'

'When I talked of your being altered by time, by the progress of years,' said John Knightley, 'I meant to imply the change of situ-

ation which time usually brings. I consider one as including the other. Time will generally lessen the interest of every attachment not within the daily circle—but that is not the change I had in view for you. As an old friend, you will allow me to hope, Miss Fairfax, that ten years hence you may have as many concentrated objects as I have.'

It was kindly said, and very far from giving offence. A pleasant 'thank you' seemed meant to laugh it off, but a blush, a quivering lip, a tear in the eye, showed that it was felt beyond a laugh. Her attention was now claimed by Mr Woodhouse, who being, according to his custom on such occasions, making the circle of his guests, and paying his particular compliments to the ladies, was ending with her—and with all his mildest urbanity, said:

'I am very sorry to hear, Miss Fairfax, of your being out this morning in the rain. Young ladies should take care of themselves.— Young ladies are delicate plants. They should take care of their health and their complexion. My dear, did you change your stockings?'

'Yes, sir, I did indeed; and I am very much obliged by your kind solicitude about me.'

'My dear Miss Fairfax, young ladies are very sure to be cared for.—I hope your good grandmamma and aunt are well. They are some of my very old friends. I wish my health allowed me to be a better neighbour. You do us a great deal of honour today, I am sure. My daughter and I are both highly sensible of your goodness, and have the greatest satisfaction in seeing you at Hartfield.'

The kind-hearted, polite old man might then sit down and feel that he had done his duty, and made every fair lady welcome and easy.

By this time, the walk in the rain had reached Mrs Elton, and her remonstrances now opened upon Jane.

'My dear Jane, what is this I hear?—Going to the post-office in the rain!—This must not be, I assure you. You sad girl, how could you do such a thing?—It is a sign that I was not there to take care of you.'

Jane very patiently assured her that she had not caught any cold.

'Oh! do tell *me*. You really are a very sad girl, and do not know how to take care of yourself.—To the post-office indeed! Mrs Weston, did you ever hear the like? You and I must positively exert our authority.'

The Cloakroom, Clifton Assembly Rooms, Bristol, by R. Sharples. A good example of the 'conversation picture' revealing dress and behaviour among the gentry.

If the Fanny Burney passage showed insights into 'manners', this extract does that and more. John Knightley is too forthright a man to care about etiquette as such. Superficially he is perhaps even disagreeable: sceptical almost to cynicism about friendship, uxorious to a fault. Though it is his way to keep people at a distance, he pays to others the respect he believes due to himself. He has the clearsighted kindness to see into the pathos of Jane's situation and to respond to it firmly, coolly, but with understanding and tact. Mr Woodhouse is very different: he has an old-fashioned, disinterested regard for ceremony—for the polite forms due from a host to a guest. Mixed with his courtly compliments to 'young ladies' and his fussiness, he has an ingenuous but genuine concern for this young lady in particular—hence his concern about the stockings. Mrs Elton—speaking across the room—is merely ostentatious. She has no rights over Jane Fairfax and no real regard for her; her interference is undesired and intrusive, but she desires to advertise herself as a masterful and benevolent lady with the status proper to the bestowal of patronage. The Burney passage illustrates the clash of social temperaments, but beyond that it has no human interest: the characters are not illuminated in their living emotions. The Jane Austen one shows three distinct attitudes to human relationships: John Knightley's intelligent feeling in association with uningratiating plainness; Mr Woodhouse's mixture of hypochrondriac egotism, disinterested ceremoniousness, and homely feeling; and the heartlessness of Mrs Elton's callous exhibitionism.

These extracts show how Jane Austen learned from her predecessors the art of prose fiction, and by assimilating their achievements, perfected her own. One feature requires a final comment: the episodes chosen from other writers for comparison with those from her own tend to be more superficially striking than those from her work. The narratives of the earlier novelists were more episodic and more extraordinary than incidents usually are in real life: all of us live experiences which are seldom of deep significance when seen in isolation, but which take on significance from their place in the web of each life seen as a whole. Living is made up of minutiae; but a minutia need not be a triviality; it was Jane Austen's perception of this, and her ability to turn the perception into imaginative insight, which give her novels their special distinctiveness.

8   The Arts and the Social Order

When one considers what has come down to us from the eighteenth-century environment, one is impressed by two qualities that distinguish it: the first is that the arts and crafts were all highly developed in accordance with a standard of taste that harmonizes them, and the second is the strongly social character of eighteenth-century taste.

To consider the first characteristic: it does not imply that eighteenth-century works have a dull uniformity. Wedgwood and Worcester china, a chair by Chippendale and one by Sheraton, portraits by Reynolds and Gainsborough, streets by Robert Adam and John Wood, a poem by Pope and one by Johnson—each of these has its distinctive qualities which are quickly recognizable by anyone who gives the matter some attention. Yet not only do the differences between works of the same kind by different artists occur within a range of common limits, but these common limits embrace works of different kinds as well.

Johnson and Pope will serve to exemplify the point that two artists—in this case poets—could each have individuality, and yet exhibit a community in their style of taste. It is not difficult to distinguish the poet who wrote

> 'Tis with our judgements as our watches, none
> Go just alike, yet each believes his own.
> POPE, *Essay on Criticism*

from the poet who wrote

> Of all the griefs that harass the distressed,
> Sure the most bitter is a scornful jest;
> JOHNSON, *London*

Pope's couplet has the flexibility and keenness of a well-handled duelling sword; it makes its comment swiftly, gracefully and precisely. Johnson's comment impresses like a heavy seal; it carries the stamp of his compassion and indignation with the weight of his personal experience. On the other hand, both are using a precisely balanced form—the couplet—and both use it with a common sense of proportion and restraint. The language is economical and lucid, and the emphasis comes with the force natural to the form, without extraneous emphasis from the writer. And these qualities of strength and elegance, restraint and precision, proportion and formal balance, recur in the architecture, the furniture, and much of the painting of the century. It is difficult to know what qualities of china and chairs two writers of the Victorian period—say Dickens and Tennyson—may have shared, unless we look into their biographies. It is not difficult to believe that Pope and Johnson would have shared many.

It was a society of collectors assured of their judgments, and of connoisseurs anxious to display. Bibliophiles who collected fine editions, linked up with antiquaries who treasured the past; these in turn encouraged collectors of prints, pictures and statues. The common interest in the art of display united the various interests—the present and the past, learning and furnishing, house and garden, town and country. The city of Bath, setting of so much of Jane Austen's two last published novels, arose anew in the eighteenth century because the architect John Wood the Elder, backed by his businesslike patron Ralph Allen, was so impressed by its Roman origins and remains that he determined to reconstruct it as a fine Roman city, and bullied the town council until in exasperated remonstrance they named after him four small streets: Be Street, Quiet Street, John Street and Wood Street. In no other century has fine street planning received such enthusiastic patronage; Bath and Edinburgh are the chief remaining monuments of it, and what is left of London squares is another.

But the patrons spent more time on their country estates than in town. Rapid developments in agricultural science made estate management very profitable to the landlords, and on their estates, too, they practised for one another's admiration their taste for display. The antiquarianism of the age played a part in this. They spread an interest in gothic remains from the Middle Ages, and for the wild nature that commonly surrounds them. Wild nature, however, is uncomfortable, and the upper classes had learned to appreciate comfort as never before. Accordingly they chose to domesticate wilderness by introducing it judiciously into their private parklands. Queen Caroline, wife of George II, for instance, decided that the new artificial lake in Hyde Park should not have the rectangular uniformity of the lakes at Versailles, but the contours of a natural one—hence the Serpentine, so-called because it curves a little. A new profession of 'improving' landscape gardeners grew up, the most famous of whom in mid century was Lancelot Brown, nicknamed

'Capability' Brown, about whom a wit said that when he got to heaven he would set about 'improving' that too.

The mention of these ornamental 'improvements' to the estates is a reminder of the strictly limited application of the word 'social' to eighteenth-century taste, or at least to the more expensive expressions of it; it was scarcely social in the sense in which we speak in the twentieth century of a 'social conscience'. There were artists— notably the painter Hogarth and his friend the novelist Fielding, who used a harsher style than we are accustomed to think of as eighteenth-century to dramatize the neglect and degradation of the poor, especially in London. But the city poor were not by tradition the responsibility of richer members of the social hierarchy in the way that the cottagers of the countryside had traditionally depended on their landlords. For the rural peasants of the eighteenth century the current term must often have sounded with an ironic ring, for the 'improvements' were often not directed where they were needed, but to the ornamental avenues and artificial lakes and ruins sur-rounding a great house.

The subject, as Alistair Duckworth has pointed out in his book on her novels, *The Improvement of the Estate*, is one of Jane Austen's themes, especially in *Mansfield Park*. In that novel, Mansfield Park itself represents established tradition, and the tradition includes a sense of responsibility, as Sir Thomas points out to Henry Crawford when the latter seems to regard a clerical 'living' as merely an amenity for the incumbent. Crawford wants Edmund Bertram to 'improve' his prospective parsonage:

'. . . You are a lucky fellow. There will be work for five summers at least before the place is live-able.'

'No, no, not so bad as that. The farm-yard must be removed, I grant you; but I am not aware of any thing else. The house is by no means bad, and when the yard is removed, there may be a very tolerable approach to it.'

'The farm-yard must be cleared away entirely, and planted up to shut out the blacksmith's shop. The house must be turned to front the east instead of the north—the entrance and principal rooms. I mean must be on that side, where the view is really very pretty; I am sure it may be done. And *there* must be your approach— through what is at present the garden. You must make you a new garden at what is now the back of the house; which will be giving it the best aspect in the world—sloping to the south-east. The ground seems precisely formed for it . . . The meadows beyond what *will be* the garden, as well as what now *is*, sweeping round from the lane I stood in to the north-east, that is, to the principal road through the village, must all be laid together of course; very pretty meadows they are, finely sprinkled with timber. They belong to the living, I suppose. If not, you must purchase them. Then the stream—something must be done with the stream; but I could not quite determine what. I had two or three ideas.'

'And I have two or three ideas also,' said Edmund, 'and one of them is that very little of your plan for Thornton Lacey will ever be put in practice . . . I think the house and premises may be made comfortable, and given the air of a gentleman's residence without any very heavy expense, and that must suffice me; and I hope may suffice all who care about me.'

Miss Crawford, a little suspicious and resentful of a certain tone of voice and a certain half-look attending the last expression of his hope, made a hasty finish of her dealings with William Price, and securing his knave at an exorbitant rate, exclaimed, 'There, I will stake my last like a woman of spirit. No cold prudence for me. I am not born to sit still and do nothing. If I lose the game, it shall not be from not striving for it.'

Mary Crawford, in other words, is determined to get Edmund, but determined to get him at his full social value, with no nonsense about moderate expense, or duties to his parishioners, or making minimum changes in an established building on the grounds that it is adequate as it is. Her brother's plans for improving the place, as Alistair Duckworth points out, are very similar to those of the famous improver, Humphry Repton, for Harlestone Hall, the house commonly considered to be Jane Austen's model for Mansfield Park. Repton was Capability Brown's successor as the fashionable improver of the age. He began by following Brown's principles, but later he tried to counteract the more fanciful tendencies of Brown's landscaping and to adapt his designs more to the character of the existing landscape and its functions. He was, however, very much in the hands of his clients, and these were not such men as Sir Thomas Bertram, who wanted no improvements even such as are required by the theatricals in his house, but rather such as Mr Rushworth of Sotherton Court, whose daughter is to marry him.

'. . . I declare when I got back to Sotherton yesterday, it looked like a prison—quite a dismal old prison.'

'Oh! for shame!' cried Mrs Norris. 'A prison, indeed! Sotherton Court is the noblest old place in the world.'

'It wants improvement, ma'am, beyond anything. I never saw a place that wanted so much improvement in my life; and it is so forlorn, that I do not know what can be done with it.'

'No wonder that Mr Rushworth should think so at present,' said Mrs Grant to Mrs Norris, with a smile; 'but depend upon it, Sotherton will have *every* improvement in time which his heart can desire.'

'I must try to do something with it,' said Mr Rushworth, 'but I

do not know what. I hope I shall have some good friend to help me.'
'Your best friend upon such an occasion,' said Miss Bertram, calmly, 'would be Mr Repton, I imagine.'

'That is what I was thinking of. As he has done so well by Smith, I think I had better have him at once. His terms are five guineas a day.'

'Well, and if they were *ten*,' cried Mrs Norris, 'I am sure *you* need not regard it. The expense need not be any impediment. If I were you, I should not think of the expense . . .'

Attitudes to improvement divide the characters very significantly; those who are in favour of it seem at first to have little in common. Rushworth is an empty-minded fop whose chief preoccupation in the theatricals is not his part (which he is unable to learn) but the clothes he is to wear—an extension of landscape improvement to costume improvement. Mrs Norris is a fussy, arrogant little woman with small ideas and large pretensions, and the Crawfords are charming, witty, and worldly-wise. But their common interest is that the reason for social living is display; each is constitutionally unable to see that relationships must have the dimension of inner depth—that social relationships are nothing if they are not implicit in personal relationships. The passage just quoted contains cunning ironies: Mrs Grant means that Maria will be the improvement Sotherton needs, but Mr Rushworth needs Maria—and she needs him—much on the same level of 'need' as his need of Repton, and that is the only sense in which 'a friend' is intelligible to him.

Gilpin and the Picturesque

Jane Austen used Repton chiefly as a satirical device, intelligible to her contemporaries, although it needs some explanation now. William Gilpin (1724–1804) was another influential mind in the sphere of eighteenth-century taste, and she used him differently—as a formative influence on her own art.

He was a man like her own father—a highly cultivated village clergyman, in her own county of Hampshire. He was a great doer of good works, a writer of moral fables and tales, and an amateur of the graphic arts; but the source of his contemporary fame was his guidebooks to scenery in the New Forest, the Peak, Wales, the Lakes and the Scottish Highlands. We have seen that eighteenth-century antiquarianism created interest in the Middle Ages, and hence in gothic ruins and the wild landscape that often surrounds them. This new enthusiasm did not stop with those who were rich enough to introduce carefully controlled wildernesses into their own estates; it aroused a wholly new and much wider attraction to landscape for its own sake. Gilpin knew that the tourists wanted some guidance in

their expeditions, and he also knew that a taste for beauty in nature is related to a taste for pictures, from which indeed it might receive its first stimulus. Consequently he used the term 'picturesque' not just for what is beautiful in nature, but for 'that peculiar kind of beauty, which is agreeable in a picture'. 'Nature', he pointed out in his *Three Essays* (1792), 'is always great in design, but unequal in composition. She is an admirable colourist; and can harmonize her tints with infinite variety, and inimitable beauty: but is seldom correct in composition, as to produce an harmonious whole.' It is odd to speak of nature as of a talented artist who has missed some basic training. But it is Gilpin's way of showing that his purpose is really dual: he is educating his readers in the appreciation of nature by making them look at it in terms of pictures, and he is also educating them in the appreciation of art, by making them look at nature as though they are artists.

As an educator in art appreciation, Gilpin has great merits. He is very conscious of the medium, whether pencil, paint, or language, and knows how a medium ought not to be used. Thus in the *Three Essays*:

> Language, like light, is a medium; and the true philosophic stile, like light from a north window, exhibits objects clearly, and distinctly, without soliciting attention to itself . . . The stile of some writers resembles a bright light placed between the eye, and the thing to be looked at. The light shews itself; and hides the object: and, it must be allowed, the execution of some painters is as impertinent, as the stile of some writers.

Here we have the reason for Jane Austen's own studied plainness of expression. As a model, she may have used Defoe, but Gilpin is reinforcing the lesson.

In another passage, he reminds us of the material out of which she composed her novels. In his essay 'On Picturesque Travel', he writes:

> Some artists, when they give their imagination play, let it loose among uncommon scenes—such as perhaps never existed: whereas the nearer they approach the simple standard of nature in its more beautiful forms, the more admirable their fictions will appear. It is thus in writing romances. The correct taste cannot bear those unnatural situations in which heroes and heroines are often placed,

Sketches by Humphrey Repton on how to improve the prospect from a small house—his own. He got permission to take in part of the road. The lower illustration shows the removal of importunate beggars; the concealment of the butcher's shop by a climbing rose; the disappearance of the cackling geese on what had been a small village green.

whereas a story *naturally* and, of course, affectingly told, either with pen or pencil, though known to be a fiction, is considered as a transcript from nature; and takes possession of the heart. The *marvellous* disgusts the sober imagination: which is gratified only with the pure characters of nature.

This might be a declaration of principle by Jane Austen herself. Just so she shows that the experiences of characters who are found to be entirely usual in their circumstances are more poignant than those whose circumstances strike one as exceptional. Richardson's Clarissa and Fanny Burney's Evelina affect us not by the extravagance of their adventures but by the extent to which they remain natural young women in spite of them; Jane Austen demonstrates that the adventures themselves are the better for being 'natural'.

Gilpin does not often direct his remarks to the act of writing, but his typically eighteenth-century tendency to discern common principles behind different arts often makes his remarks about the graphic media applicable to the literary ones. For example, in the 'Essay on Prints' he discusses the best way for an artist to present the characters in a picture of a literary or legendary episode in terms that might apply to a narrative:

He must introduce them properly. They should be ordered in so advantageous a manner, that the principal figures, those which are most concerned in the action, should catch the eye *first*, and engage it most. This is very essential in a well-told story. In the first place, they should be the least embarrassed of the group. This alone gives them distinction. But they must be farther distinguished, sometimes by a *broad* light; sometimes by a *strong shadow*, in the midst of a light; sometimes by a remarkable action, or expression; and sometimes by a combination of two or three of these modes of distinction.

It is not difficult to apply such visual terms to Jane Austen's novels; she herself does so when she writes to her sister about *Pride and Prejudice*: 'The work is rather too light, and bright, and sparkling; it wants shade.' Gilpin's prescriptions for introducing characters are born out by her practice. *Pride and Prejudice* is an example. In the first two chapters we are shown the Bennet family as a group, responding variously to the news of Mr Bingley's arrival in the neighbourhood; the chapters are short, and already in Chapter 3 we are in the 'broad light' of the ball. Here Elizabeth is 'disembarrassed' of her sisters and separated from the company (despite the novelist's own disparaging comment) by being shown in 'a strong shadow'—that is to say, she is obliged to sit out a dance owing to 'the scarcity of gentlemen'. Moreover, she is forced to overhear Mr Darcy's disdainful remarks about the qualities of the young ladies, and specifically about her own inadequacy. Jane Bennet is also 'disembarrassed' by being singled out by Mr Bingley as 'the most beautiful creature I ever beheld'; but Jane is set back in perspective so as to take second place in the composition, both here and throughout the book. After the ball, Elizabeth's reactions to Darcy's haughtiness are spirited and strong; she emerges into a strong light, and becomes distinguished by her wit and positive character ('remarkable action or expression'). It is Darcy who is now to be distinguished by shadow—the shadow of disrepute and uncertainty that surrounds his reputation—until they come together in a common radiance. The third of the sisters to achieve prominence in the story has already been slightly but sufficiently accentuated at the end of Chapter 2, by the remark which characterizes her dangerous mixture of crudity and self-assurance: 'Oh,' said Lydia, stoutly, 'I am not afraid; for though I am the youngest, I am the tallest.'

F. W. Bradbrook (in *Jane Austen and Her Predecessors*), remarking on the relevance of Gilpin's writings to her art, points out that critics of the novels commonly use Gilpin's pictorial vocabulary without, apparently, associating it with Gilpin himself. This is itself an indication of how well she assimilated his conception of artistic organization. His terms include 'composition', 'repose', 'design', 'disposition', 'expression', 'effect', 'spirit', 'execution', 'catching lights', 'contrast', 'keeping' (i.e. 'different degrees of strength and faintness, which objects receive from nearness and distance'), and 'perspective'. In the 'Essay on Prints' he carefully defines them, and there are few that cannot be used, in accordance with his definitions, in describing Jane Austen's methods. Of course he did not originate them, and most have remained current in art criticism. Their particular significance in connection with Jane Austen is related to Gilpin's endeavour to use them in order to translate wild nature, with its confusion, into a composition; to get irregularity into order and harmony without falsifying it. The novelist must similarly represent human nature in a composition without falsifying it but yet enabling the reader to receive the experience of it as a whole.

Jane Austen's particular problem was that the English novelists who preceded her had not yet achieved a form adequate to the enterprise. They had sometimes presented experience as real but unordered; this is a criticism which might be made specifically against Defoe. Sometimes they had ordered experience in such a way that the narrative inhibited the representation of natural life. *Tom Jones*, for instance, is a fine narrative structure, but ill-adapted to the conveyance of subjective experience. Or they had introduced characteristics which belong to the licensed improbabilities of romance—a criticism which could be made of Richardson and Fanny Burney. Gilpin's lessons in perspective, composition, design and harmony were what Jane Austen needed to give the novel form its status as a fully serious art form, intelligible to common experience and at the same time apprehensible as a judgment of that experience; in short, what Matthew Arnold was later to say great poetry should be, 'a criticism of life'.

The problem was, however, not just to gain shapeliness and coherence for the novel. The phrase I have just used, 'intelligible to common experience', implies a limitation on shapeliness, on what Edmund Burke called 'smoothness', which for him was one of the qualities of true beauty. Gilpin asserted that picturesque beauty, on the contrary, required 'roughness' or 'ruggedness'. Truth in art is not the same as truth in philosophy: 'A truth is a truth, whether delivered in the language of a philosopher, or a peasant: and the *intellect* receives it as such. But the artist, who deals in lines, surfaces, and colours, which are an immediate address to the eye, conceives the very truth in his *mode* of representing it.' Gilpin is here distinguishing the graphic artist from the writer, but he is thinking of the latter as the sort of didactic writer that he was himself. The counsel he gives to the graphic artist is equally relevant to the imaginative writer, if for 'eye' we substitute 'imagination', and it fits in well with his concept of 'roughness' as an element of the picturesque. He makes the opposite concept of 'smoothness' include 'neatness' and formality: a Palladian building (such as the large English country houses of the period) he remarks, may be beautiful in itself, but it is merely a dead, formal object in a picture. One of the defects of the heroines—and still more of some of the heroes—of eighteenth-century novels had been their tendency to resemble, in their moral idealization, the formality of the grand Palladian building. Physically, it would be more appropriate to compare them with the carefully qualified idealizations made by Gainsborough in his full-length portraits of fashionable young women. Both kinds of idealization Jane Austen sought to defy in the presentation of her heroines.

One may illustrate the difference in her art by comparing the descriptions of two heroines by their lovers—one from Richardson's *Clarissa*, and the other from *Mansfield Park*. In the first, Lovelace is describing Clarissa to his friend Belford.

> Thou hast often heard me launch out in praise of her complexion. I never beheld in my life a skin so illustrously fair. The lily and the driven snow is nonsense to talk of: her lawn and her laces one might indeed compare to those: but what a whited wall would a woman appear to be, who had a complexion which could justify such unnatural comparisons? But this lady is all glowing, all charming flesh and blood; yet so clear, that every meandering vein is to be seen, in all the lovely parts of which custom permits to be visible.
>
> Thou hast heard me also describe the wavy ringlets of her shiny

hair, needing neither art nor powder; of itself an ornament, defying all other ornaments; wantoning in and about a neck that is beautiful beyond description.

Her head-dress as a Brussels-lace mob, peculiarly adapted to the charming air and turn of her features. A sky-blue riband illustrated that. But, although the weather was somewhat sharp, she had not on either hat or hood. (vol. iii, Letter 5)

Lovelace goes on to describe at some length the rest of Clarissa's dress. Gilpin would perhaps have approved of this; there is the element of what he called 'roughness' in the glowing flesh and the 'wantoning' hair. But, apart from the description being all superlative, and the clothes too immaculate (they are on horseback—but Richardson's heroines are seldom anything but well-dressed in any predicament), the portrait is surely too 'framed', too free from commonplace circumstances to convey a 'normal' woman. Compare this with Henry Crawford's description of Fanny Price in Chapter 30:

'Had you seen her this morning, Mary,' he continued, 'attending with such ineffable sweetness and patience, to all the demands of her aunt's stupidity, working with her, and for her, her colour beautifully heightened as she leant over the work, then returning to her seat to finish a note which she was previously engaged in writing for that stupid woman's service, and all this with such unpretending gentleness, so much as if it were a matter of course that she was not to have a moment at her own command, her hair arranged as neatly as it always is, and one little curl falling forward as she wrote, which she now and then shook back, and in the midst of all this, still speaking to *me*, or listening, and as if she liked to listen to what I said. Had you seen her so, Mary, you would not have implied the possibility of her power over my heart ever ceasing.'

There is nothing awesome or idealized in this portrait; even though Henry's depiction of Fanny's sweetness and patience is of qualities quite out of the ordinary, they are shown at work unselfconsciously in an ordinary context. Jane Austen's heroine is within our own physical space, whereas Richardson's is still suspended on the wall of romance.

9   Women in Life and Literature

Anna has not a chance of escape ... Poor Animal, she will be worn
out before she is thirty.—I am very sorry for her.—Mrs Clement too
is in that way again. I am quite tired of so many Children.—Mrs Benn
has a 13th.

JANE AUSTEN to her niece Fanny, 1817

Anything is to be preferred or endured rather than marrying without
affection.

JANE AUSTEN to Fanny, 1814

Anna was the daughter of Jane Austen's eldest brother, James: her
mother, Anne, had died in her infancy. Four of Jane Austen's brothers
married twice, and a fifth (Edward) remained a widower after his wife
had died young. And yet, ten days earlier than the letter to Fanny
in 1817, she had written: 'Single women have a dreadful propensity
for being poor—which is one very strong argument in favour of
Matrimony.'

If we put the three quotations together, we get a sombre impression
of the lot of women in Jane Austen's lifetime. With fairly rare exceptions, only two professions were open to them—the stage, and teaching; the former offered few opportunities and enormous risks, and the
latter was arduous, penurious, and little respected. There were also, of
course, literature and journalism, but they seldom afforded a stable
livelihood. Unless, like Emma Woodhouse, a woman had a private
income, happy matrimony was the only way of life in which middle-
and upper-class women could normally hope to find themselves satisfied, esteemed, and secure. But limited mobility restricted choice; it did
not do to be romantic or fastidious, as Charlotte Lucas, in *Pride and
Prejudice*, realizes when she accepts an offer from Mr Collins.

In some respects, the social predicament of women was worse in the
eighteenth century than it had ever been, not because their opportunities for employment were fewer than in previous periods but because
they were becoming steadily more informed and more inclined to
think for themselves. Their education was typically unsystematic, but
more and more current literature, onwards from the journalism of
the *Spectator* in the reign of Queen Anne, was addressed as much to a
female readership as to a male one; thus women—and some men—
increasingly questioned the assumption that they were intellectually
inferior. Before the century opened, Daniel Defoe wrote: 'I have often
thought of it as one of the most barbarous customs in the world, that we
deny the advantages of learning to women.' But what exasperated

women who did acquire such advantages was the dislike men were inclined to display towards the acquisition. Thus, near the middle of the century, Pope's friend and enemy, Lady Mary Wortley Montagu, wrote in a letter:

> I do not complain of men for having engrossed the government. In excluding us from all degrees of power they preserve us from many fatigues, many dangers and perhaps many crimes. But I think it the highest injustice to be debarred the entertainment of my closet, and that the same studies which raise the character of a man should hurt that of a woman. We are educated in the grossest ignorance, and no art omitted to stifle our natural reason. If some few get above their nurse's instructions, our knowledge must rest concealed and be as useless to the world as gold in a mine.

Lady Mary is here alluding not merely to male prejudice against the education of women's minds, but to the prejudice against the exhibition of learning by women should they happen to acquire any. The writers of moral instruction for girls were firm about this. Mrs Chapone in 1773 (*Letters on the Improvement of the Mind*) and Dr Gregory in 1774 (*A Father's Letters to his Daughter*) both insisted not so much that learning was unnecessary, although they were highly selective in what should be learnt, as that the display of it gave offence.

The prevalence of this prejudice against women having an intellect has led David Monaghan, writing on 'Jane Austen and the Position of Women' (in *Jane Austen in a Social Context*) to declare that 'Women can rarely have been held in lower esteem than they were at the end of the eighteenth century'. However, the wide and forcible expression of a prejudice indicates some kind of provocation from fact: it may be not so much that women were held in lower esteem in the period as that some writers thought there were dangerous indications of women getting above themselves. The remarkable lives of two of Jane Austen's contemporaries, middle-class women of contrasting opinions, are perhaps evidence that such uneasiness had cause. Hannah More (1745–1833) was a woman of frail physique who nevertheless had a triple career of great public fame. She was first a writer with a reputation for wit and accomplishment, a close friend of the most famous literati and artists of her day—Samuel Johnson, Horace Walpole, David Garrick, Joshua Reynolds; in this phase she published volumes of esteemed poetry and wrote a very successful tragedy (*Percy*, 1777) produced on the London stage by Garrick. She then became a leading Evangelical, a member of the famous Clapham sect, and a friend of such leading reformers as William Wilberforce who led the movement against the slave trade; in this capacity she wrote numerous moral tales with vast circulation, the most celebrated being *Coelebs in Search of a Wife* (1809) which Jane Austen was so reluctant to read. Her third career was as an active philanthropist, founding schools for the children of labourers in the neglected area of Somerset where she lived, arousing and overruling the hostility of their employers in the process. Although this activity stimulated accusations that she was dangerously radical, her beliefs were in fact strongly conservative, and much of her writing during the French Revolution was directed against its sympathizers in England. One such sympathizer was the other striking example of feminine individualism in the period—Mary Wollstonecraft (1759–97). Like Hannah More, she began her independent life with the establishment of a school, but then she engaged in a kind of journalistic activity very unusual for contemporary women by writing for the *Analytical Review* run by the radical publisher Joseph Johnson. In 1792 she published her *Vindication of the Rights of Woman*, protesting against the traditional assumptions about female characteristics, such as timidity and submissiveness to male authority, arguing for much greater openness to women in the professions and commerce, and affirming the superiority of poor women who maintained their families in hardship over gentlewomen who were morally enfeebled by their education in useless accomplishments. However, it was the independence of her conduct and opinions which made her notorious when they became known through the publication by her husband, William Godwin, of his *Memoir* of her, a year after her death in giving birth to the child who was to become Mary Shelley, the author of *Frankenstein*. Like Hannah More, she acquired the friendship and respect of some of the leading intellectuals of the time, though her associates were such as Hannah More vigorously opposed. And yet, mutually hostile though they were, the two women were alike in their energy, courage and independence, contrasting with the constraints under which even the most privileged women of their society were expected to live. They had in common that the eventfulness of their lives was certainly very different from the uneventfulness of Jane Austen's. Despite that difference, it is not altogether surprising that some critics of her work have sought in it affinities with both. Like them, she lived in a period in which women were in much greater numbers forming independent judgments, whether or not they were feminist in sympathy or actively unconventional in their conduct.

Mary Wollstonecraft and Hannah More resemble two sides of a frame for the image of woman among Jane Austen's contemporaries; if we are to complete the frame we need to consider, in addition to these opposed exceptions, what habit and tradition expected of women, especially among the more privileged classes. Seen from this viewpoint, what compensation did women have for their double deprivation—of the right to earn their economic independence, and to be acknowledged as the intellectual equals of men? A dubious one was the power which they were acknowledged to possess over men's emotions. 'You have stronger influences', wrote Lord Halifax in 1688, 'than all our *Privileges* and *Jurisdictions* can pretend to have against you.

You have more strength in your *Looks*, than we have in our *Laws*, and more power by your Tears, than we have by our Arguments.' It was not so much individual women, however, who possessed these powers, as a kind of abstract deity, 'Woman'. But 'Woman' represented one kind of deity for the man of pleasure who was quite willing to ruin any number of individual women in the course of a lifetime of lamenting his enslavement to 'the sex', and another for the moralist in the Puritan tradition, for whom Woman was practically the guardian of man's conscience by her scrupulous defence of virtue against the unruliness of human passion.

Such a moralist was Samuel Richardson. The moralist who is also a novelist does not necessarily speak with different voices in accordance with which of the two roles happens to come uppermost; if he or she has the calibre of a George Eliot or a Leo Tolstoy the functions will be unified. In Richardson they were not, so that while Pamela Andrews is vividly portrayed so long as she is resisting the lechery of Mr B., she becomes a tedious and unreal embodiment of the feminine ideal once she has married him. In *Clarissa Harlowe* the novelist triumphs over the moralist for most of the novel, but arguably the impressiveness of the story is due less to the portrayal of the heroine, who is sometimes inordinately idealized, than to that of the villain. Lovelace is the 'man of pleasure' who does not believe in the reality of the moralist's 'pure woman', but on the contrary that all women surrender their virtue once they are offered sufficient inducement. Yet the ruthlessness with which he pursues and persecutes Clarissa indicates that his real desire is to prove to himself that she really is as pure as she seems; that just for once the beauty of a woman is really matched by the truthfulness of her virtue. It is not that he cares for virtue as such. He is 'Lovelace' because he is 'loveless', unloving but also unloved, and secretly yearning to be loved wholly and disinterestedly. The moralist in Richardson meant the tragedy of his novel to arise from the conflict between a man dedicated to libertinism and a woman dedicated to virtue; the novelist made it more complex. Lovelace cannot cease the persecution of Clarissa until he is convinced of her virtue, but since there is no point at which a truth can be proved to a man who fundamentally despairs of believing it, so there is no point at which Lovelace can stop short until he has brought Clarissa to her death.

What Richardson indirectly reveals in his masterpiece is an attitude which had become habitual: women were not so much interesting for themselves, psychologically—though, in fairness, it cannot be said that he ignores Clarissa's psychology—as for the mystiques imposed on them, whether these were to see them as symbols of inexhaustible pleasure or as moral emblems. It was an attitude derived from long traditions of romantic love and sexual comedy countered by a shorter one of Puritan admonition. The minds of the eighteenth century could not ignore the traditions and doctrines of the seventeenth, but the temper of the age was different. Moderate and rational, seeking proportion in all things, the more liberal thinkers of the early eighteenth century opposed the harshness of Puritan ethics, modified the libertinism of the Restoration reaction against it, and reasoned against the pessimistic philosophy of the seventeenth-century political philosopher Thomas Hobbes, with his belief that human beings are fundamentally non-moral and guided only by self-interest. A leading thinker of this new kind was Anthony Ashley Cooper, third Earl of Shaftesbury (1671–1713), whose *Characteristics of Men, Manners, Opinions, Times* was published in 1711. He is now little read, but in his own century he was a leading influence not merely in Britain but on the Continent. In particular he is relevant to our purposes because, according to an essay by the twentieth-century philosopher Professor Gilbert Ryle (in *Critical Essays on Jane Austen*, edited by Southam) he may have exercised a deep influence on Jane Austen.

Shaftesbury set himself to refute Hobbes, and he also gave an alternative view of human nature to that of puritanism. He acknowledged that man is a bundle of appetites and emotions, but he argued that the world was not a jungle of competing interests, but a work of art that proceeded from the mind of God. Nature is thus a harmony of varied and opposing qualities, and it followed that for him human nature should be comparably balanced and harmonious:

> The balance of Europe, of trade, of power, is strictly sought after, while few have heard of the balance of their passions, or thought of holding these scales even . . . we should then see beauty and decorum here, as well as elsewhere in Nature; and the order of the moral world would equal that of the natural.

He further argued that just as human beings have an aesthetic sense which enables them to appreciate natural beauty, so they possess a moral sense which, in the healthy mind, impels it to seek such a balance. He has little to say about women as such, but one of his characters (the essays are written in the form of dialogues in reported speech) is scathing about the 'foppish, courtly humour' which made it a practice to 'deify the sex' and 'raise them to a capacity above what Nature had allowed, and treat them with a respect which in the natural way of love they themselves were the aptest to complain of'. On the moral plane at least, women, he implies, are level with men, and are not to be set up either as the objects of masculine passion, or as the embodiments of moral ideals.

We do not know whether Jane Austen read Shaftesbury; Gilbert Ryle has argued that there are signs in her work that she did, and he is certainly an author whom she would be likely to find in her father's library. What we can say is that his philosophy of balance, and his tendency to bring moral feeling into accord with aesthetic feeling, would both have been congenial to her. There is, for instance, an affinity between her titles *Pride and Prejudice, Sense and Sensibility*, and such a passage from Shaftesbury as this:

> Fain would I have persuaded you to think with more equality of Nature, and to proportion her defects a little better. My notion was, that the grievance lay not altogether in one part, as you placed it, but that everything had its share of inconvenience: pleasure and pain, beauty and deformity, good and ill, seemed to me everywhere interwoven; and one with another made, I thought, a pretty mixture, agreeable enough in the main.

Equally important would have been his emphasis on the moral significance of the beauty of nature, and his attitude to women. But Jane Austen was certainly a more serious and interesting moralist than Shaftesbury. Her attitude to morality was not less flexible, but it was less relaxed. The novels concern the difficulties, perils, and indispensability of self-discovery which alone make possible the achievement of a true self-discovery. There is an underlying sternness in her fiction which owes more to Richardson than to Shaftesbury; Richardson, after all, with all his limitations, did expound the feminine temperament and its predicament in moral issues more deeply than any other writer of his time. The virtues which she insists on her heroines possessing or acquiring—candour of heart, balance of judgment, sensitivity of feeling—amount to what Shaftesbury seems to have meant by the fruits of a properly cultivated 'moral sense'. But more than any of these she valued true understanding of moral principle for its influence on human development, and in this respect she was aware, as he was not, of the influence of social deprivation on the moral character, at least in regard to the disadvantages suffered by women in the eighteenth century.

The Predicament of the Jane Austen Heroine

All the heroines find themselves suffering under overlapping disadvantages in four categories: material, family, social, and personal. Each category varies in importance from book to book.

Thus the material disadvantage is not very considerable in Northanger Abbey: Catherine Morland is discovered to be less rich than she was supposed to be. In *Sense and Sensibility* the family are morally, though not legally, defrauded through the effects of the antiquated law of entail, according to which the estate must descend to the nearest male heir, leaving the widowed Mrs Dashwood and her two daughters on the edge of poverty. In *Pride and Prejudice* poverty is a future menace, and an entail is again the cause; the Bennet girls will see their father's estate pass to their cousin, Mr Collins—hence Mrs Bennet's fluster and obsession with the problem of how to marry them off, if not profitably, at least securely. In *Mansfield Park* Fanny Price is a poor relation who has to endure, at best condescending patronage, and at worst oppression. Emma in the next novel has no material difficulties but this turns out to be itself an important source of her personal and social problems. In *Persuasion* Anne Elliot, the second daughter of a baronet who lives above his means, is no financial catch, but this blends with her family problem that she has refused the man she loves from counsels of prudence, and yet is allowed no voice in the family financial affairs, about which she alone has the necessary sense of proportion.

When one turns to the families one notices the curious fact that there are no satisfactory parents in Jane Austen's novels. In three of them—*Sense and Sensibility*, *Emma*, and *Persuasion*—one parent is dead, and the survivor is inadequate. In *Northanger Abbey* Catherine is temporarily in the care of substitute parents throughout the story; one of these, Mr Allen, is too self-preoccupied to take care of her interests, and his wife is too foolish. The same, but more evidently, is true of the real parents of the Bennet girls, and of the substitute ones—her uncle and aunt—of Fanny Price. It is curious, too, that in four of the novels, an important part of the heroine's problem is the deprivation of her natural home, although this is only temporarily true of Catherine Morland, who is merely on holiday from hers. In the remaining two, the Bennet girls have to look forward to the loss of their home, and, once again, Emma's sense of safe establishment is one source of her confused values.

It may appear that Jane Austen constructed unnecessary difficulties for her heroines, thus bringing an element of arbitrariness into her stories. But reflection will show, first, that these 'accidents' are not improbable in themselves: parents died prematurely more often in those days, and it has never been unusual for young people, at some stage, to be thrust out of their natural environment. Secondly, the effect of these breaks in the continuity of their safe development is to bring into relief the predicament of the young woman of the time. Educated unsystematically if at all, not expected to cultivate independence of mind, they depend on wise, balanced, continuous protectiveness if they were to grow up as persons. (The balance was important: Emma Woodhouse's predicament was that, with a father whom she could dominate and no mother to restrain her, she was *too* secure.) The break in the continuity of their protective circumstances tended to frustrate their destinies and to transform them into social objects with (always excepting Emma) small, or at least reduced, commodity value. They are not responsible for their predicaments, and have no initiative in remedying them; they are 'objects' in so far as the marriage market and good fortune seem likely to determine their material and social survival.

In their relationships to their surrounding societies and to themselves, on the other hand, they have a limited initiative. They cannot choose whom they will meet, but they have power over their discernment and behaviour which will do much to decide who will want to meet them. Their domestic and material circumstances, as well as their innate temperaments, will predispose them to handle themselves and their relationships in certain ways, which initially handicap their progress, but which eventually, through experience, they learn to correct. Elizabeth Bennet, to take one example, has an independence of mind and a disposition to take control of her relationships which derive from the inertia of her father, the foolishness of her mother, the intelligence she inherits from the former, and the active temperament she inherits from the latter. Someone has to take sensible decisions and to moderate foolish ones, and the very absence of a strong directive force in her family incites her to exert herself in these ways. But this very positiveness and independence incline her—given the smallness of the provincial world in which she has grown up—to premature judgments or 'prejudices' when she herself and her pride are threatened.

The Jane Austen heroine has to live from her personal resources in a space which has confined them and offers her little scope: yet happiness and fulfilment are achieved. The art of the novels lies in showing how they are achieved against the weight of improbability.

Part Three
The Art of Jane Austen

10 Characterization: Heroines and Heroes

'. . . To be so bent on Marriage—to pursue a Man merely for the sake of situation—is a sort of thing that shocks me; I cannot understand it. Poverty is a great evil, but to a woman of Education & feeling it ought not, it cannot be the greatest.—I would rather be Teacher at a school (and I can think of nothing worse) than marry a Man I did not like.'— 'I would rather do any thing than be Teacher at a school—said her sister. *I* have been at school, Emma & know what a Life they lead; *you* never have.—I should not like marrying a disagreeable Man any more than yourself,—but I do not think there *are* many very disagreeable Men;—I think I could like any good humoured Man with a comfortable Income.—I suppose my Aunt brought you up to be rather refined.' 'Indeed, I do not know.—My conduct must tell you how I have been brought up. I am no judge of it myself . . .' '—But I can see in a great many things that you are very refined. I have observed it ever since you came home, & I am afraid it will not be for your happiness. Penelope will laugh at you very much.'

JANE AUSTEN, *The Watsons*

The Watsons is an unfinished sketch of a novel, written in 1803 and abandoned, according to a great-niece, on the death of Jane Austen's father. The Watsons are a poor family by the standards of their class, consisting of an invalid and widowed father, three daughters, and two sons. Emma Watson has been brought up away from her family by an aunt for fourteen years, and has only returned to it at the age of nineteen. The dialogue takes place while the eldest daughter is driving Emma, who is the youngest, to her first ball. There she is to win the devotion of a boy of ten by dancing with him when he has been disappointed by another young woman who does not consider promises to little boys to be binding.

> . . . he stood the picture of disappointment, with crimson'd cheeks, quivering lips, & eyes bent on the floor. His mother, stifling her own mortification, tried to sooth his, with the prospect of Miss Osborne's second promise;—but tho' he contrived to utter with an effort of Boyish Bravery 'Oh! I do not mind it'—it was very evident by the unceasing agitation of his features that he minded it as much as ever.—Emma did not think, or reflect;—she felt & acted—. 'I shall be very happy to dance with you Sir, if you like it.' said she, holding out her hand with the most unaffected good humour.

We have learnt that Emma Watson is poor, that she attaches importance to 'education and feeling', that her eldest sister considers her 'refined'; she is also too proud to hunt men merely to secure a husband with a good income, and it seems that this sort of pride has much to do with what her sister calls her 'refinement'. It is not, at all events, the sort of pride that despises a small boy as a dancing partner, nor, as it turns out, is it of the kind that might incite her to respond to the advances of the town dandy, with whom all the girls are supposed to be infatuated, nor even those of the local peer, who, according to Austen records, was later to propose to her and be refused. What her sister calls refinement appears to mean placing personal preferences based on the private feelings above the opportunities of social security and prestige.

The antagonists to what is personal, sincere, and sensitive are of two kinds: the crude vices of affectation, unscrupulousness, and arrogance, and also the more subtle weaknesses of misjudgment and ignorance of the self. The first sort implies what is merely social (in opposition to the personal) and the second implies confusion between them. Both sorts occur throughout Jane Austen's novels; the earlier ones (up to and including *Pride and Prejudice*) emphasize the cruder antagonists; the last three are more concerned with the subtler ones.

Disingenuousness, arrogance and unscrupulousness are qualities especially associated with those whose main aim is 'to get on' in society. *Lady Susan*, another early and unpublished work, is the only one which has this kind of character at the centre of the story. Unlike *The Watsons*, it is completed, and is written in letters. Lady Susan is a widow of thirty-five, with great personal charm and no scruples at all; she has a daughter of marriageable age whom she first neglects, then suppresses, and finally tries to marry off to a rich nincompoop whom she eventually marries herself. Just as it is the daughter's problem that her mother entirely controls her, so it is the problem of the Emma Watsons of society that it tends to be the Lady Susans who are in control there, too. Society constitutes the conditions in which the individual has to live, and it is the individuals with the most dedicated ambitions and the hardest hearts who are likely to control those conditions. The vulnerable are opposed to the ruthless, and in the Jane Austen theatre, the vulnerable come off best. It is one of her principal problems to show not only how this can happen, but that it is right and natural for it to happen.

Pump Room, Bath. The scene of incidents in Northanger Abbey. *The chief Bath inn, the White Hart, where the Musgroves stay in* Persuasion, *stood opposite the Pump Room.*

The stage is always small, and the cast corresponds, though it is never quite as scanty as the '3 or 4 Families in a Country Village', which Jane Austen told her niece Anna was 'the very thing to work on'. Moreover, the moral design is much more varied than the restricted setting and social range seem to allow. This variety arises from the novelist's use of three distinct ways of 'learning' people, each of them natural to the experience of non-fictional life. The first is the way in which we learn ourselves, partly by self-discovery and partly through enrichment of relationship; the second is learning by the discovery of our misjudgments how to arrive at true judgments of those who strongly influence us; and the third is the way in which we register the characteristics of those for whom we do not deeply care, but with whose idiosyncrasies we have to live.

The first category, and part of the second, relate to the heroines' experience of themselves and to their experience of their lovers—the heroes; about both of these we shall speak later. The rest of the second category—the subjects of misjudgment—are composed of what I choose to call the 'prime antagonists' to the heroine, since 'villain' does not seem appropriate to describe them. Thus General Tilney is the antagonist to Catherine Morland in *Northanger Abbey*; Willoughby to Marianne Dashwood in *Sense and Sensibility*; Wickham to Elizabeth Bennet in *Pride and Prejudice*; the Crawfords to Fanny Price in *Mansfield Park*; Frank Churchill to Emma Woodhouse; and Mr Elliot to Anne Elliot in *Persuasion*. The antagonist is not necessarily hostile to the heroine—usually, indeed, the contrary—nor necessarily even opposed to the heroine's desires. He or she is antagonistic in the subtler sense of confusing the assumptions, values or principles of the heroine (or of someone important to her) in such a way that they either frustrate the heroine's growth to self-knowledge, as in the instance of Frank Churchill in his relationship with Emma, or stand in the way of the fruition of the heroine's destiny, as the Crawfords stand in the way of Fanny Price. In each case the antagonist is to some extent dark or confusing to the reader as well as to the heroine or to other characters, but the reader is always given clues to a right judgment, whether or not they are available to the heroine as well.

The Caricatures

The characters which belong to the third class offer much less difficulty to the reader, inasmuch as they have marked characteristics of a simple kind, and do not usually develop unexpected traits in the course of the story (though there are a few notable exceptions). These qualities of unaltering distinctness and simplicity perhaps justify us in labelling them 'caricatures', so long as we do not confuse caricatures with the grotesques which other people's caricatures sometimes are. They are much the most numerous of the three groups, and include Isabella and John Thorpe in *Northanger Abbey*; Lucy Steele, Robert Ferrars, John Dashwood and his wife, and Mrs Jennings and her daughters in *Sense and Sensibility*; Mrs Bennet, Mary and Lydia Bennet, Mr Collins and Lady Catherine de Burgh in *Pride and Prejudice*; Mrs Norris, Lady Bertram, and Mr Rushworth in *Mansfield Park*; the Eltons and Miss Bates in *Emma*, and Anne's father, Sir Walter Elliot, in *Persuasion*. These caricatures are mostly (not always—Miss Bates is a prominent exception) disagreeable as well as invariably comic, and they are also often more hostile to the heroine than those I have labelled 'the prime antagonists'. But the heroine is not usually mistaken about them (it is a measure of Catherine Morland's ingenuousness that she can be deceived by the false friendship of Isabella Thorpe) and the reader never is. Moreover, if they are hostile, they are usually more a nuisance than really dangerous: Mrs Norris, for example, makes Fanny's life a misery, but she has no real power (whereas Mary Crawford has) to influence Fanny's destiny, although she tries to.

An important effect of the caricatures is to parody, or act as foils to, the central characters, whose qualities are thereby thrown into stronger light, either by being seen in comic exaggeration or by force of contrast. Thus Isabella Thorpe's affectation of friendly devotion and her spurious enthusiasm for romances throw into relief the sincere ardours and naïve romantic indulgences of Catherine Morland. In *Sense and Sensibility*, Mrs Palmer's delight that her husband, for all his hatred of her, cannot escape his marriage, is a kind of nightmarish good sense: after all, she makes what should be a horribly unhappy union into a source of satisfaction for herself. She parodies the real good sense of Elinor Dashwood, as her sister, Lady Middleton, whose refinement scarcely tolerates any conversation in case it should turn vulgar, but who regards it as a privilege for visitors to be plagued by her darling children, parodies the sensibility of Marianne. In *Mansfield Park*, Mrs Norris parodies Fanny Price in their situations and contrasts with her in character: both are poor relations and virtual dependants, although Mrs Norris has fastened herself on the Bertrams whereas Fanny is forcibly transferred to them. Mrs Norris obsequiously flatters the Bertrams; Fanny subjects herself to them devotedly and with a genuine humility. Fanny spends her life being really useful; Mrs Norris spends hers talking about being so. Finally, Mrs Norris makes great claims to being needed by the Bertrams and for a long time imposes this illusion on them, but the illusion wears steadily thinner until at last they are glad to get her out of the house to make a home for the disgraced Maria, with whom she ends her days in mutual strife. Fanny, on the other hand, begins by being adopted in a spirit of pure benevolence, but by the end of the book she has not only

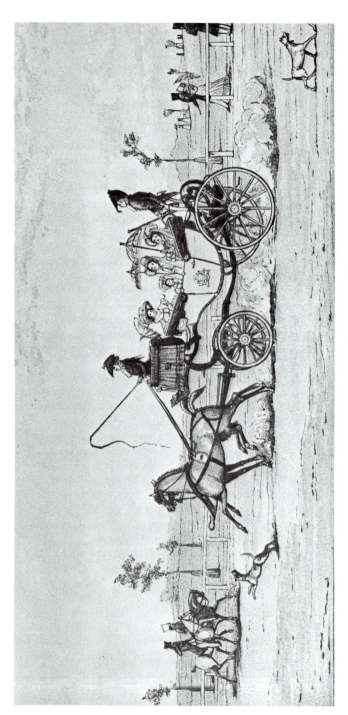

A barouche, a fashionable style of vehicle favoured by smart ladies such as Mrs Elton in Emma

become indispensable to her uncle and aunt, but marries Edmund to live with him in mutual harmony and devotion. Thus Jane Austen uses caricature not only to reinforce the distinguishing qualities of her main characters, but also as an element of composition, contrasting, in Gilpin's terminology, the 'rough' with the 'smooth'.

Minor Characters

She is true to the principles of Gilpin also in her delineation of those minor characters who shade off from the caricatures; whose roles do not warrant the force of caricature. These are placed, as Gilpin would have put it, 'in keeping'. He defined 'keeping' as 'different degrees of strength and faintness, which objects receive from nearness and distance'. In a novel, a 'distant' character is one that remains in the background of the story, and must therefore be kept in a background perspective. A minor but exacting task for any novelist is to imbue such characters with enough life but not too much: if they have too little, the reader has the uncomfortable sense of a small but worrying blankness in the composition; if they have too much, they will distract attention from those who ought to be concentrating it. On the whole, Jane Austen has remarkable control over this process of dimming out the characters as they recede from the centre. For example, in *Mansfield Park* Maria and Julia Bertram are never far from the foreground of the story because they have a necessary though secondary importance to it. We are made aware of their self-willed natures, their strong but immature emotions, their competitiveness and mutual jealousy; they are something more than caricatures, but they are not allowed any depth of complexity. Behind them is the agreeable but slight caricature of Mr Rushworth, Maria's foolish and foppish fiancé. Fainter still is their brother Tom, who shows a masculine version of their restless, superficial energies without their motives for competition and jealousy. Then, quite in the background, there is the Crawfords' half-sister, Mrs Grant, endlessly patient with her selfish husband who hardly appears in person at all, and perpetually goodnatured, whether as hostess to her relatives or as a volunteer for a small but necessary part in the aborted play. As the characters recede, they are carefully possessed of fewer and less attention catching features of temperament, but very seldom are they allowed to fade into total colourlessness. Perhaps only in the incompletely revised *Persuasion* do we find a failure of that kind, in the character of Mrs Smith.

The Heroines

On the other hand the fullness of the central character—the heroine— in a Jane Austen novel is such that many readers find it difficult to receive fully what the novelist is conveying to them. The difficulty is the greater because, unlike the caricatures, the character of the heroine is not static; it grows and unfolds, sometimes in two directions—by critical self-discovery on the one hand, and on the other by the slow fruition of innate virtues. Catherine Morland, Marianne Dashwood, Elizabeth Bennet, to a less extent Fanny Price, and above all Emma Woodhouse—all these grow through both processes; Elinor Dashwood and Anne Elliot (perhaps the most delicately portrayed of all the heroines) exhibit the slow fruition alone. This ripening of the virtue is the ripening of the self; the heroines do not 'possess' their virtues but are the virtues. Because the virtue is intrinsic, the ripening occurs to some extent involuntarily, despite, or even because of, the circumstances, which are invariably unpropitious. For the same reason—the intrinsicality—the virtues exhibit two qualities; the first is endurance even through disappointment amounting almost to despair, and the second is outgoingness, or generosity; the virtue is not hoarded for personal satisfaction or exhibited merely for public admiration, but communicates itself like a marvellous gift. Jane Austen is a great moralist because she understood (as Fielding did, and as Shaftesbury preached) that either a virtue communicates itself or it—and the personality itself—is nothing.

Catherine Morland in *Northanger Abbey* exemplifies this generosity, in the brief scene in which she begs forgiveness at the theatre for having apparently ignored the Tilneys' invitation and gone out with the Thorpes instead.

The play concluded, the curtain fell; Henry Tilney was no longer to be seen where he had hitherto sat, but his father remained, and perhaps he might be now coming round to their box. She was right: in a few minutes he appeared, and making his way through the then thinning rows, spoke with like calm and politeness to Mrs Allen and her friend. Not with such calmness was he answered by the latter. 'Oh, Mr Tilney, I have been quite wild to speak to you, and make my apologies. You must have thought me so rude; but indeed it was not my fault. Was it Mrs Allen? Did not they tell me that Mr Tilney and his sister were gone out in a phaeton together? and then what could I do? But I had ten thousand times rather have been with you. Now, had not I, Mrs Allen?

'My dear, you tumble my gown,' was Mrs Allen's reply. Her assurance, however, standing sole as it did, was not thrown away; it brought a more cordial, more natural smile into his countenance, and he replied in a tone which retained only a little affected reserve, 'We were much obliged to you, at any rate, for wishing us a pleasant walk after our passing you in Argyle Street. You were so kind as to look back on purpose.'

A curricle, a light carriage, analagous to a modern sports car, such as John Thorpe is vain of in Northanger Abbey

'But indeed, I did not wish you a pleasant walk, I never thought of such a thing; but I begged Mr Thorpe so earnestly to stop; I called out to him as soon as ever I saw you. Now Mrs Allen did not—Oh! you were not there. But, indeed, I did; and if Mr Thorpe would only have stopped, I would have jumped out and run after you.'

Is there a Henry in the world who could be insensible to such a declaration? Henry Tilney, at least, was not. With a yet sweeter smile, he said everything that need be said of his sister's concern, regret, and dependence on Catherine's honour.

'But, Mr Tilney, why were you less generous than your sister? If she felt such confidence in my good intentions, and could suppose it to be only a mistake, why should you be so ready to take offence?'
'Me! I take offence!'
'Nay, I am sure by your look, when you came into the box, you were angry.'
'I angry! I could have no right.'
'Well, nobody would have thought you had no right, who saw your face.'
He replied by asking her to make room for him.

Catherine is totally artless: in her warmth of feeling for the Tilneys, more especially for Henry, and distress at having offended them, she tumbles over phrases and exposes her feelings nakedly to an extent that an artful girl (like Isabella Thorpe) would consider fatal to whatever might remain of Henry's regard for her. Isabella would consider that Catherine was blatantly 'throwing herself at his head', but she is not doing this, because she has no reserve of self to throw herself with; she merely surrenders in perfect candour, which is none the less for her unconsciousness of what she is doing. Henry is an intelligent but disillusioned young man, who has so far liked her because she is pretty (though with little more than the normal prettiness of youth) and unspoilt. He has expected her to get spoilt, and assumed that the Thorpes had begun the process; he now finds that she is still unspoilt, and he will find that she is unspoilable.

It is true that Catherine's naïvety puts her in danger—greater danger than she undergoes from the machinations of her false friends. The danger, however, does not arise from her ingenuous exhibition of her affections, but from her impressionability and her susceptibility to false images, especially those derived from literature. That literature, especially inferior literature, may be harmful because it may confuse the already difficult and confused relationships of real life, is one of Jane Austen's themes. The theme is most conspicuous in *Northanger Abbey*, which is partly a satire on the sensationalism of the gothic romance, but it reappears, more subtly, in three of the other novels. In *Sense and Sensibility*, Marianne Dashwood learns from the poets whom she admires to cultivate the role of a girl with a broken heart to an extent that blinds her to the same afflictions suffered by her sister Elinor, who prefers to keep hers from sight for the sake of her own and her sister's equilibrium. In *Emma*, the heroine tries to build a real life romance round her protégée, Harriet Smith, only to find that her manipulation of other people's lives involves her own destiny in such a way as to threaten her own deepest unconscious desire. In *Mansfield Park*, the characters add confusion to their already confused feelings by acting parts in a play which parody their actual relationships outside it.

The use of literature to show how it may falsify life is one aspect of the truthfulness which distinguishes Jane Austen's concern as a novelist. Another aspect is the refusal to follow her predecessors and contemporaries in glamorizing the heroine—that is to say she refuses to bestow talents and beauty which in normal experience are exceptional. And the same restraint seems to dictate her portrayal of the heroes of her novels, but even more severely. Only those of the first and last written—Henry Tilney, and Captain Wentworth in *Persuasion*—possess a normal quality of allowable charm. Those in between—Edward Ferrars, Darcy, Edmund Bertram, Knightley—seem to be deliberately subdued; at the same time the 'charmers' in the same novels—Willoughby, Wickham, Crawford, Churchill—are exposed respectively as mercenary, perfidious, unprincipled and mendacious. It is tempting to suspect a kind of puritanic perverseness behind the creation of these characters; as though the author believed that masculine charm was itself a symptom of depravity, and that masculine virtue was necessarily accompanied by a quality of temperament which is to some degree repellent to women. Before committing oneself to so disparaging an opinion, however, it is important to look more closely at the principles on which these characters are created.

The Heroes

In classifying Jane Austen's characters into three main groups, I suggested that the heroes are to be found in the second: those who deeply influence the heroine, but are open to her misjudgment because of the complexity of their natures, of their circumstances, or of both. Bearing in mind that the heroine presents the central viewpoint in the novels, so that her experience of the hero is essentially the reader's, we need then to remember that a young woman's experience of men was shaped by the social circumstances in which she met them. Those circumstances were such as to encourage in men a kind of fatuousness of behaviour: the man who was bent on winning feminine admiration would dispose his manners and appearance so as to attract them. On the other hand, the man who was too fastidious for this kind of display, or too respectful of women as people (that is, not merely regarding them as objects for flirtatious courtship) to indulge in it, would naturally retreat behind some kind of gravity or reserve. Jane Austen's kind of society thus made it difficult for girls to get to know men; they could meet their own sex without the presence of the other, but they could not know how men behaved among themselves, except that they might behave very differently. It follows that men were necessarily something of a mystery to young women, and that the more complex were their natures, the more mysterious they were likely to be.

Since the reader is always made to share the heroine's viewpoint, he necessarily has a less complete view of the hero than he has in a novel (for instance, by another woman novelist, George Eliot) in which the novelist ranges freely, centring the viewpoint now in this character, now in that, and sometimes withdrawing to an authorial standpoint, independent of them all. It is true that in two of the novels, the heroine begins with a special relationship with the hero: Fanny grows up with Edmund almost as with an older brother, and Mr Knightley is an established family friend of the Woodhouses. But these special relationships have the effect of inhibiting any other sort, so that Fanny is sadly aware that as Edmund's 'sister' she is never likely to be looked on by himself as a possible wife, and Emma does not consider Knightley—a kind of adopted uncle—as a possible husband, until she realizes that someone else may marry him and snatch him from her.

The heroes, then, are presented under unusual constraints. The task for the novelist would seem to be, therefore, to use what she allows to appear so as to suggest what can only be inferred. This, however, is to regard the hero as though he were an independent creation, separate from the novel of which he forms a part. A better statement of the novelist's problem is whether the hero sustains that part of the artistic structure which depends upon him. In general, it is the role of a Jane Austen hero to provoke, offset, goad, and magnetize the heroine. He may do all these. Darcy, for instance, first of all provokes Elizabeth Bennet by his frank indifference to her charms at the ball, at the same time as he offsets her family and social environment by his innate fastidiousness and evident disdain for their provinciality and vulgarity. He goads her into rage by his arrogant assumption that (in the proposal scene) he is conferring honour by culling her from this environment, while she is convinced that he has behaved with mean vindictiveness against Wickham. But all the time he magnetizes her as a human being: she discovers that he has feelings which are capable of being wounded, and that she has wounded them unjustly; that his apparent arrogance is compatible with sensitive and courteous relationships with those to whom they are due, and that he is capable of large generosity just when she would have expected him to withdraw from her and her family in understandable, if not justifiable, contempt. Darcy matches Elizabeth by his pride, prejudice, and critical spirit, but he also enlarges her, both by arousing them in apparently justified dimensions, and then bringing her proud, critical, independent faculties into harmony with the deep emotions of which he is capable, and capable of inspiring in her. Another hero, Captain Wentworth, operates in only one way: he magnetizes the heroine, Anne Elliot, by restoring to her the life of her feelings when it has seemed (at the beginning of the novel) that she is doomed to fade away, merely to be exploited, unappreciated, by the humanly inferior family which imprisons her.

Heroes and Heroines: Marriage and Money

In considering the relationship of the heroines and the heroes in the novels, it is important to emphasize the material factor which conditions, inhibits, and confuses it—that of money. A 'good' marriage, in the society Jane Austen depicts, is always one which enhances status, and status is primarily a matter of wealth. With the exception of Emma Woodhouse with her £30,000, all the heroines of the novels are short of wealth, and hers is the exception proving the rule, since it is her fortune which is the cause of her self-blinding complacency. Whereas in *Emma* the outcome of the narrative is the exposure of the heroine's fallacious materialism, in the other novels the outcome is the circumvention of the heroines' material disadvantages. The most disadvantaged is Fanny Price in *Mansfield Park*; she is dependent on her uncle by marriage, Sir Thomas Bertram, and the opening paragraph is a pungent summary of the social attitudes conditioning her background:

> About thirty years ago, Miss Maria Ward of Huntingdon, with only seven thousand pounds, had the good luck to captivate Sir Thomas Bertram, of Mansfield Park, in the county of Northampton, and to be thereby raised to the rank of a baronet's lady, with all the comforts and consequences of an handsome house and large income. All Huntingdon exclaimed on the greatness of the match, and her uncle, the lawyer, himself, allowed her to be at least three thousand pounds short of any equitable claim to it. She had two sisters to be benefited by her elevation; and such of their acquaintance as thought Miss Ward and Miss Frances quite as handsome as Miss Maria, did not scruple to predict their marrying with almost equal advantage. But there certainly are not so many men of large fortune in the world, as there are pretty women to deserve them. Miss Ward, at the end of half a dozen years, found herself obliged to be attached to the Rev.

Mr. Norris, a friend of her brother-in-law, with scarcely any private fortune, and Miss Frances fared yet worse ... Miss Frances married, in the common phrase, to disoblige her family, and by fixing on a Lieutenant of Marines, without education, fortune, or connections, did it very thoroughly.

Fanny, the daughter of the lieutenant, is in effect a Cinderella, and her two cousins, the daughters of Sir Thomas who adopts her, are the 'Ugly Sisters'—in their arrogant treatment of her if not in their appearance. The Cinderella theme is also applicable to *Pride and Prejudice*, in which Elizabeth Bennet wins Mr Darcy, the rich Prince, out of the clutches of Mr Bingley's two sisters. From the point of view of Mr Darcy, in spite of all his prejudices against marriage into a lower status, one can see that he is too discriminating to be blinded by the arrogance of the Bingley women, and learns to appreciate the lively (though prejudiced) independence of Elizabeth in spite of the silliness and vulgarity of her mother and sister Lydia. For the worldly Mary Crawford in *Mansfield Park*, 'Matrimony was her object, provided she could marry well' (chapter 4), and 'marrying well' required status (with its accompanying wealth) as much as personal value, but Darcy comes to see that 'status' is of no consequence by comparison with personal value in maintaining the dignity of his stock. The distinction is not a matter of romantic preference, about which Jane Austen is ironical; it is an irony that in *Sense and Sensibility* it is the 'sensible' sister, Elinor, who marries dangerously by bringing her 'sensible' lover Edward Ferrars into disfavour (albeit temporary) with his worldly mother, whereas her romantic sister ends by marrying safely after near ruin by her romantic lover. Jane Austen does not support romantic love in opposition to worldly wisdom; Anne Elliot in *Persuasion* never considers that she had been wrong to refuse her lover's first offer on prudent advice, although it has threatened her with the deprivation of her lasting happiness. On the other hand she is perpetually concerned to show that mere worldliness is as foolish as mere romanticism, and to disentangle from personal relations the mere worldliness which obscures and distorts them.

11   The Construction of the Novels

'. . . You have a very smiling scene before you.' 'Do you mean literally or figuratively? Literally I conclude. Yes, certainly, the sun shines and the park looks very cheerful. But unluckily that iron gate, that ha-ha, give me a feeling of restraint and hardship. I cannot get out, as the starling said.' As she spoke, and it was with expression, she walked to the gate; he followed her. 'Mr Rushworth is so long fetching the key!'

JANE AUSTEN, *Mansfield Park*, Chapter 9

The Fable of the Starling

The starling to which Maria Bertram refers comes into Sterne's *Sentimental Journey*. He finds it in a cage hanging above a Paris passageway, while he is pondering the evil of the Bastille. He has just decided that confinement there is mainly under the control of the mind:

'Tis true, said I, correcting the proposition—the Bastile is not an evil to be despised—But strip it of its towers—fill up the fossé—un-barricade the doors—call it simply a confinement, and suppose 'tis some tyrant of a distemper—and not of a man, which holds you in it—the evil vanishes, and you bear the other half without complaint.

Then the talking starling's pathetic cry disturbs him; he tries to release it, but the door of the cage is so enmeshed with wire that he fails. The bird haunts him as an image of what it is really like to be imprisoned. However, he acquires it and discovers its history. It turns out that an English groom had rescued it as a helpless fledgeling, learned to love it, bought the cage for it, and taught it to speak the sentence—which, being in English, was not understood by its present French owners, nor, of course, by the bird itself. Sterne tells the story to an English peer, who craves the bird as a gift. From him it passes half way round the House of Lords and then into the Commons: 'But as all these wanted to *get in*—and my bird wanted to *get out*—he had almost as little store set by him in London as in Paris.' But did the bird want to get out or not? Would it have been kind to release it to a freedom which it had never known? What is the truth about freedom and imprisonment?

Maria chooses to interpret Henry Crawford's 'smiling scene' literally, and not figuratively as he plainly intends. She does not love Mr Rushworth, to whom she is engaged, but expects him to release her from that gilded cage of cold principle, Mansfield Park, by making her mistress of Sotherton. Whether marriage with Mr Rushworth will prove to be just another, though different, cage, is a question she does not choose to discuss, sitting as she is with a man to whom she is genuinely attracted. But Henry Crawford suggests that they can escape from their literal confinement by squeezing round the edge of the gate:

'I think it might be done, if you really wished to be more at large, and could allow yourself to think it not prohibited.'
'Prohibited! Nonsense! I certainly can get out that way, and I will . . .'

—so they do, just as later she is to make her escape from marriage to Mr Rushworth by eloping with Henry Crawford, and paying for that defiance of prohibition by a life sentence with her Annt Norris.

In this episode, Fanny is also present. She has a succession of companions besides Maria and Henry: first, Mary Crawford and Edmund, then Julia, and last, Mr Rushworth. All of them make their escape, but she remains, having no one who wants her company and no one she dares to pursue. She is very much more the starling than Maria Bertram; taken, like the bird, as a fledgeling, rescued from an overcrowded nest, and placed under the gaolership of Aunt Norris. But does she want to escape, and what would freedom mean to her? Certainly her home nest at Portsmouth, when she returns to it, proves to be a worse cage than spacious and orderly Mansfield Park. The problems of 'getting out', of how not to make a false escape from a psychologically confining space, of how to achieve release of the entire self, neither betraying the feelings by surrendering them to the judgment, nor betraying the judgment by false feelings—these are the deepest themes of Jane Austen's novels.

The problems are above all presented through a special use of language—Jane Austen's celebrated use of irony, by which what happens and exists is described in terms of what seems, but in such a way that there is an evident incompatibility between the appearance and the truth. What can be described as so right is betrayed by the very description as so wrong; for instance, Maria Bertram's wedding:

It was a very proper wedding. The bride was elegantly dressed—the two bridesmaids were duly inferior—her father gave her away—her mother stood with salts in her hand, expecting to be agitated—her aunt ready to cry—and the service was impressively read by Dr Grant. Nothing could be objected to when it came under the discussion of the neighbourhood, except that the carriage which conveyed the bride and bridegroom and Julia from the church door to Sotherton, was the same chaise which Mr

Rushworth had used for a twelvemonth before. In everything else the etiquette of the day might stand the strictest investigation.

The wedding is what Maria wanted, but its heartlessness implies the marriage from which she runs away.

Maria's mind was so obsessed with the obvious solution—marriage—that she took no account of other realities which had a bearing upon it, for instance whether she could be satisfied with the mere status conferred on her by Mr Rushworth's wealth. Mrs Bennet is likewise obsessed with the single idea. *Pride and Prejudice* opens with the celebrated sentence: 'It is a truth universally acknowledged, that a single man in possession of a good fortune must be in want of a wife.' F. W. Bradbrook has suggested that Jane Austen may be parodying a rather pompous remark by Addison in *Spectator 413*. Addison refers to 'that great Modern Discovery, which is at present universally acknowledged by all the Enquirers into Natural Philosophy: namely, that light and colour, as apprehended by the imagination, are only ideas in the mind, and not qualities that have any existence in matter'. If so, her allusion to that sentence is apt, for just as our impressions of light and colour are none the less sure even if they are subjective, so Mrs Bennet's expectations of Bingley would not be stronger if it were positively known that he was using Meryton as his wife-hunting ground.

On Mrs Bennet's side, it must be admitted that her one desire for her daughters to make socially prestigious marriages was in line with her society. In that society, too, the foolish Mrs Bennets were perfectly tolerated. Local society was confined and strict; those who were fit to meet socially could not be avoided on other grounds. If on the other hand one chose to go outside the socially acceptable circle, this was likely to mean that one subjected oneself to the outspoken contempt of trivial but overbearing snobs like Sir Walter Elliot:

> 'Westgate Buildings!' said he; 'and who is Miss Anne Elliot to be visiting Westgate Buildings? A Mrs Smith. A widow Mrs Smith: and who was her husband? One of the five thousand Mr Smiths whose names are to be met with everywhere. And what is her attraction? That she is old and sickly. Upon my word, Miss Anne Elliot, you have the most extraordinary taste! Everything that revolts other people, low company, paltry rooms, foul air, disgusting associations, are inviting to you . . .'

The irony of Sir Walter speaking these words is evident, because we know by now that he has nothing to recommend him as a human being beyond his title; he is a man who, we are told in the very first sentence of the novel, 'for his own amusement, never took up any book but the *Baronetage*.' More insidious, because more plausibly expressed, are the essentially similar opinions of his relative, the heir to the baronetcy, William Elliot:

> 'My idea of good company, Mr Elliot, is the company of clever, well-informed people, who have a great deal of conversation; that is what I call good company.'
> 'You are mistaken,' said he gently, 'that is not good company; that is the best. Good company requires only birth, education, and manners, and with regard to education is not very nice.'

He is trying to persuade Anne that it is not a waste of her life to cultivate her father's inane but titled relatives, of whom Sir Walter is so proud. There is little evident irony in the fact that he should express such practical, blatant worldliness; it at least seems an honest, and, in terms of that society, realistic opinion. But when, a few chapters later, we learn from Mrs Smith the self-seeking motives for his cultivation of Sir Walter, this speech reads differently. Mr Elliot has the merit of being genuinely in love with Anne, but otherwise he is not what he seems; his opinion is the intriguing sophistry of an intelligent bounder.

Narrative Construction

A Jane Austen novel proceeds in two phases. In the first, the heroine is shown in her original circumstances: her family, natural or substituted; her circle of acquaintances; her economic advantages or disadvantages. Above all, we are shown her basic temperament, and the qualities of her nature which make for her happiness in this environment. In this phase the irony is cheerful and overt; the intriguers, if there are any, are ingenuous rather than ingenious; it is usually not yet clear to what fatalities the heroine's nature is endangering her. The first phase, in brief, exhibits the heroine surrounded by the bars of her cage. The second phase begins with the appearance of the character or characters whom I have termed in the previous section the 'primary antagonists'—the intriguers in every novel: General Tilney, Lucy Steele and Willoughby, Wickham, the Crawfords, Churchill, William Elliot. This phase also brings to a crisis whatever in the heroine's nature constitutes an obstacle to her favourable destiny. The effect of both elements is usually, first, to make the heroine aware of her confinement, or of the painfulness of it, as never before, and secondly to make the confinement seem inevitable and permanent just when she is developing urgent desires for release. When, for instance, Wickham runs away with Lydia Bennet, Elizabeth and Darcy would seem to be finally lost to each other.

However, another process has also been at work. Besides the trivialities, pretentiousness, affectation, intrigue and misunder-

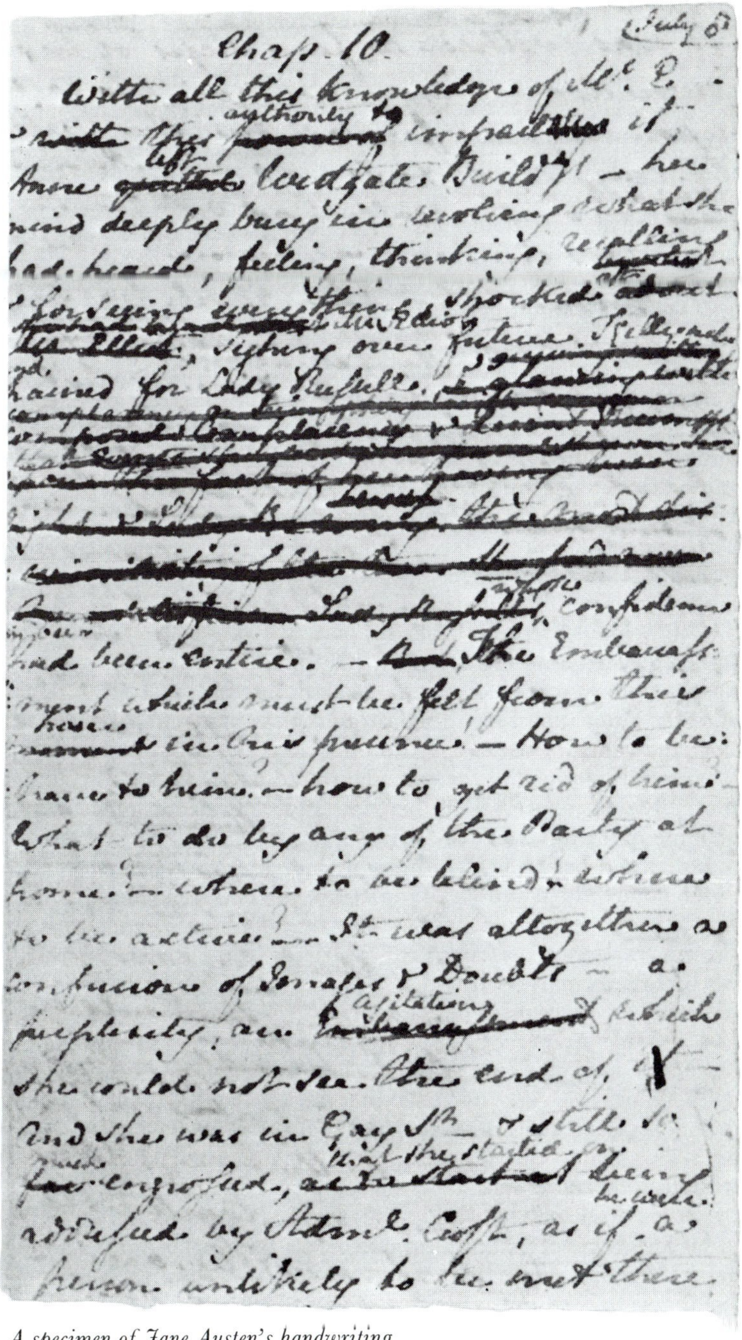

A specimen of Jane Austen's handwriting

standing—what we may call the gainseeking upper current of the story—there has been a deepening and broadening of the heroine's, sometimes also the hero's, understanding and sympathy. Even when (in *Pride and Prejudice*) the feelings of the hero and heroine were first aroused antagonistically, the very antagonism first precludes indifference, and is then transfigured into admiration, finally into love, when each has come to realize how deeply each has misjudged the other. The new understanding, with all the feeling that has accumulated behind it, transforms catastrophe into opportunity. So Lydia's disgrace, instead of constituting the final rupture between Darcy and Elizabeth, becomes the pretext for destroying the barriers between them. When (in *Mansfield Park*) there has been no antagonism, or even estrangement, between the hero and the heroine, but only a long delay in the fruition of their relationship, the catastrophe (in this case Maria's disgrace) brings Edmund's awakening: he is able at last to distinguish between his emotion for Mary, which has caused division in his nature, from the truth about his feelings for Fanny, whose love heals and integrates him.

Thus in each of the novels society is set in opposition to true personal relationship. Society sets constraints on the individual, and also offers deceitful opportunities of escape from these constraints. The individual has to discover his own way of release. First he has to recognize the deceits for what they are. Then he must reach a deeper understanding of mutual relationship than society as such can offer—not abolishing the constraints but making them irrelevant, since they do not exist to constrain this inner freedom of love.

Society is opposed to the personal in the novels because it tempts the individual to seek the superficial and factitious in place of the genuine and deep, but it is never opposed as such, as a system of manners and behaviour to which the individual is expected to conform. Some odd paradoxes result from this independence (neither hostility nor subjection) of personal relationship as Jane Austen presents it. In *Sense and Sensibility*, Marianne is the romantic heroine who wants to marry without deference to society's prejudices, but her romantic lover plays her false because he loves money too much, and it is her prudent sister Elinor, and Elinor's very unromantic lover who make the 'romantic' match (he is cast off by his family) while Marianne ends by marrying the safe and reliable Colonel Brandon. Marianne's mistake is not that she wants her marriage to be a love match or nothing, but that she insists on behaving as though the social circumstances are unreal. Elinor and Edward, on the other hand, marry because they love each other, in indifference to his family's indignation, but not before they can find a means of living together above the level of misery. In *Emma*, the heroine's social snobbery at the beginning of the novel causes the disruption of her protégée's engagement to a modest farmer; at the end, Harriet

Smith is allowed to return to her farmer, and we see that Emma's interference was mistaken, not only on personal grounds but, in spite of her snobbery, on grounds of social propriety as well. There is no reason, in the world of the novels, why what is personally right should not be socially right also; what is shown to be essential is that the personal should take priority over the social, not the other way round—but this does not mean that the social circumstances should be (or can be) totally disregarded.

Settings: the Ritual Entertainments

All the same, although society is not, as such, defied by the novelist, she shows it imposing the conditions which severely restrict the protagonists' self-discovery and discovery of each other. They meet only under the restraints of socially realistic settings, which prescribe the etiquettes and limits of communication between them. The settings usually receive little descriptive attention, although we know where we are and why, but Jane Austen always gauges with precision the importance of the occasion. Outstanding among such occasions is some kind of public assembly, usually a ball. Balls were obviously heightened occasions, when characters from the different circles in the novel could all be collected together, when the young women were expected to make a special display of themselves, and the young men either made the special advances that were expected of them, or were equally conspicuous when they did not. Usually they mark crises in the heroine's relationships, and occur with significant regularity either near the beginning of the story or at a critical point rather more than half way through. In Chapter 3 of *Northanger Abbey*, Catherine Morland meets Henry Tilney at a ball; in Chapter 28 of *Sense and Sensibility*, Marianne receives her mysterious and heartbreaking rebuff from Willoughby at one. Elizabeth is rebuffed by Darcy at the ball in Chapter 3 of *Pride and Prejudice*; the ball in Chapter 28 of *Mansfield Park*, when Fanny Price 'comes out', precedes Henry Crawford's offer of marriage to her. In *Emma*, the ball in Chapter 38 is the occasion when Harriet Smith, to Emma's consternation, begins to imagine Mr Knightley to be in love with her. In *Persuasion* (Chapter 20) a public concert is used instead of a ball; it brings to a crisis the rivalry for Anne of Mr Elliot and Captain Wentworth.

On the whole, public assemblies are used as occasions for causing misunderstandings, or bringing to a climax unhappy if necessary crises, in the heroine's career. They are occasions when genuine intimacy is most difficult and wrong conclusions are most likely to be drawn. The triumph of the intimate over the public is more likely to occur in the open air, as when Elizabeth and Darcy begin a new understanding when they meet in his park at Pemberley, or Anne

Elliot and Captain Wentworth walk up through the streets of Bath at the end of *Persuasion*. The most notable of such scenes of explanation in the open, however, is perhaps Chapter 49 of *Emma*, not so much because the scene is rich in itself, as because it culminates what many consider to be the richest and closest textured of all the six novels.

The Meaning of the Fable

Before proceeding to an examination of that novel, I would like to conclude this section by referring again to Sterne's fable of the starling. Maria's reference to it is the only one in Jane Austen's writings; one has no right to assume that it made a strong impression on her. And yet the episode does seem to cast an indirect light on her conception of freedom, and its attainment by her sex in the society into which she was born.

Four points about the starling episode are worth illustrative emphasis. The first is that Sterne initially persuades himself that freedom is mainly a state of mind; it is the sight of the bird that changes his opinion. The second is that the groom did not buy the cage to torture the bird, but as an act of protective love, because he wanted to keep it. The third is similar: the groom taught his bird to say 'I cannot get out' not out of cruelty but as a joke, because it is natural to assume that a caged bird would want to escape. Yet this is not necessarily true (if it is, imprisonment would probably kill it) and in any case the starling does not understand the words it is mimicking. The fourth point is that that the words are not understood either by its later human owners—the French because they do not understand English, and the English because, as Sterne facetiously says, they are too engaged in getting in (to Parliament, ministries, the peerage) to feel any true sympathy with its pathetic appeal.

The application of these points is especially relevant to *Mansfield Park*, and in particular to its heroine. She, as I have mentioned, is the starling if anyone is: she is encaged by an act of charity, and reminded hourly of her dependence by Mrs Norris; she has an affectionate nature whose deepest need is to feel loved, but she is forced to be satisfied with the condescending, cousinly affection of the one man who, as she feels, could release her emotionally. She makes pathetic appeals to him in the language she supposes appropriate to share her emotions ('Here's harmony, here's repose . . .')

but Edmund only reflects that she has learnt her lesson well, and forgets his promise to let her out under the night sky. Yet, many readers insist, if Fanny had really wanted freedom, it was Henry Crawford who could have given it to her much better than Edmund Bertram, and him she refuses. The reason for her refusal is that Henry's freedom—the flighty indulgence of feelings by responding to worldly enticements—is not hers. For Fanny freedom *is* a state of mind, one to be rested in, a permanence, wholeness, and consistency of feeling centring on one place and one person; Mansfield Park (with its order and principle but redeemed from its worldliness) and Edmund, with his devotion to these fixities and to her. The other characters, especially Mary Crawford, are all too concerned with getting into the world to understand Fanny's abhorrence of it.

If we consider the fable of the starling in relation to the novels as a collection, we should first observe that Jane Austen has two kinds of heroine—the outgoing and the withdrawn, who alternate in the successive books. Catherine Morland, Elizabeth Bennet, and Emma Woodhouse are the outgoing heroines; Elinor Dashwood, Fanny Price, and Anne Elliot, the withdrawn ones. Their problems are complementary. The outgoing heroines have more to learn, because an active nature is inclined to take its mind uncritically for granted. The withdrawn heroines have more to resist, since the world tolerates withdrawal only if it can equate it to voluntary self-extinction. Or in terms of Sterne's fable of the starling as I have interpreted it, the outgoing heroine has to learn the meaning of the bird's cry 'I cannot get out', to recognize from what she has to liberate herself, since Sterne was partly right in his first opinion that freedom and imprisonment have much to do with the state of mind. The withdrawn heroine, on the other hand, has to learn that her imprisonment is a reality, that withdrawal into the inner world is not freedom but death, unless the self thus disengaged can give itself and thus relate itself to kindred selves without.

12 *Emma*

Seldom, very seldom, does complete truth belong to any human discourse . . .

Emma, Chapter 49

The fourth in order of publication of Jane Austen's novels and the fifth in order of writing, *Emma* was published in three volumes in December 1815 and dated 1816 by the publisher, John Murray. The 'order of writing' of the novels is, however, a contentious subject: on the one hand critics have assumed that *Emma* was written entire in 1814 after the completion of *Mansfield Park*, and on the other hand Mrs Leavis has reasoned that it was a slow development over the years from the early fragment entitled *The Watsons*, probably written in 1803.

The setting is a characteristic one: a 'large and prosperous village' called Highbury, supposed to be situated sixteen miles from London and nine from Richmond, in Surrey. Emma Woodhouse and her father live on the edge of this village in what is evidently its principal house, named Hartfield. Just up the road at Randalls lives Mr Weston, a family friend, married to Emma's former governess whom old Mr Woodhouse persists in calling 'poor Miss Taylor', in spite of her contented marriage, because she had once been happily ensconced in his own household and he dislikes change. A mile away is Donwell Abbey, an old country mansion belonging to George Knightley, another family friend; he is the principal landowner of the neighbourhood and his large estate borders the Woodhouses' small one. Emma's sister Isabella is married happily to John Knightley, Mr Knightley's brother. Looking inwards to the village, we are told that 'the Woodhouses were first in consequence there'. There is the young, as yet unmarried vicar, Mr Elton, and the middle-aged spinster daughter of a previous vicar, Miss Bates, who lives in genteel poverty with her widowed mother. Beyond these society fades to the fringes of the Woodhouse visiting circle and beyond: there is Mr Cole who has retired from trade, Mr Perry the apothecary, Mr Coxe the lawyer, Mrs Goddard who keeps a school— but from Mrs Goddard's school one other major character emerges. This is Harriet Smith, 'the natural daughter of somebody'—a somebody whom Emma, to satisfy her imagination, assumes to be a gentleman, so that she can justify herself in her scheme to restore Harriet to what she considers must be her proper social rank. The other major characters not yet mentioned all come from beyond

Highbury and its neighbourhood; they enter the novel after rather more than a third of its course, although the advent of each is heralded by gossip and discussion. Miss Bates's impoverished orphan niece, Jane Fairfax, first appears in person in Chapter 20. Mr Weston has a son by a former marriage, adopted by a rich aunt and obliged to take the aunt's surname of Churchill; after several postponements, Frank Churchill arrives to visit his father in Chapter 23. The young vicar marries, and brings his wife to Highbury in Chapter 32.

Emma stands apart from the other novels in at least one respect. Whereas the heroines of the other novels are all to some extent disadvantaged in a worldly sense, Emma Woodhouse starts with every worldly advantage. She is 'handsome, clever, and rich', and she has other advantages as well. One of them, since families are usually embarrassments in Jane Austen, is that she scarcely has one. Her mother's death happened too long ago even to be a sad memory, and her semi-invalid father so dotes on her as to resemble an amenable child. Her elder sister, Isabella, is as gentle and pliable as Mr Woodhouse, and is in any case out of the way; so is her former governess, Mrs Weston, who had been a substitute mother of a kind but had always indulged Emma rather than guided her. Thus, at the age of nearly twenty-one, Emma rules her parental household and all her immediate circle; there is no one in it (except, as we shall see, Mr Knightley) to challenge her strong will and good intelligence, and no one who does not love and admire her. In addition, she is the queen of local society.

With so little obstruction to the serene movement of her life, and so little commensurate with her active nature and abilities, it might seem that Emma's main risk would be boredom. But this is not so: boredom is only for fools. She stands at a shop door, contentedly watching the small incidents of the village street, for 'a mind lively and at ease, can do with seeing nothing, and can see nothing that does not answer' (Chapter 27). Indeed, in a sense her problems arise from the opposite of boredom, for there is no danger of her ceasing to be active. In a conversation with Harriet Smith in Chapter 10, she expounds the strengths of her temperament, and at the same time unconsciously exposes the fearful risks she is in danger of running; she has just been explaining that she sees no need for herself ever to marry:

> 'Dear me! but what shall you do? How shall you employ yourself when you grow old?'
> 'If I know myself, Harriet, mine is an active, busy mind, with a

Polesden Lacey, Surrey, the alleged original of Hartfield, the home of Emma Woodhouse in Emma

great many independent resources; and I do not perceive why I should be more in want of employment at forty and fifty than at one-and-twenty. Woman's usual occupations of eye, and hand, and mind, will be as open to me then as they are now, or with no important variation. If I draw less, I shall read more; if I give up music, I shall take to carpet-work. And as for objects of interest, objects for the affections, which is really the great evil in *not* marrying, I shall be very well off, with all the children I love so much, to care about. There will be enough of them, in all probability, to supply every sort of sensation that declining life can need. There will be enough for every hope and fear; and though my attachment to none can equal that of a parent, it suits my ideas of comfort better than what is warmer and blinder. My nephews and nieces!—I shall often have a niece with me.'

(Chapter 10)

In isolation, this speech may stimulate little comment, except perhaps it strikes rather disagreeably. The tone is smug: one pictures the middle-aged woman mapping out her day—always busy, but always occupied with activities which are chosen because the time must be filled, because they are 'woman's usual occupations', not because of any inner impulse. But if we take the passage in the context of all that we come to know about Emma and her circumstances, it is much worse. We already know by Chapter 10 that Emma's propensity is to interfere; that in the very act of speaking she is trying to shape the thoughts and feelings of Harriet Smith; we come to know that Emma's nephews and nieces have, or will have, parents who would be the very worst subjects for interference with their children. Emma's sister, Isabella Knightley, is a doting mother, and she is also the sort of person who is incapable of denying a request; John Knightley is on the other hand a very positive man, equally devoted to his family life, but intolerant of interference and interruptions in it. Isabella would never refuse Emma's repeated demands for a niece, and her husband would never forgive her for submitting to them; if anything could fracture the John Knightley marriage, it would be the middle-aged Emma. 'If I know myself . . .' In one sense she knows herself only too well, but she does not understand herself.

At this point in the story, Emma has already gone far in her project of shaping the fortunes of her protégée, Harriet Smith. Harriet is the 'natural daughter of somebody', and has attracted her attention because 'her beauty happened to be of the sort which Emma particularly admired'. Emma is a romantic. Sure (since she can see nothing wanting to her own good fortune) that she is debarred from having a romance herself, she is determined to arrange one for Harriet, but, since Emma is also very practical, it is to be a romance with a substantial goal.

Those soft blue eyes and all those natural graces should not be wasted on the inferior society of Highbury and its connexions. The acquaintance she had already formed were unworthy of her. The friends from whom she had just parted, though very good sort of people, must be doing her harm. They were a family of the name of Martin, whom Emma well knew by character, as renting a large farm of Mr Knightley, and residing in the parish of Donwell—very creditably, she believed—she knew Mr Knightley thought highly of them; but they must be coarse and unpolished, and very unfit to be the intimates of a girl who wanted only a little more knowledge and elegance to be quite perfect. *She* would notice her; she would improve her; she would detach her from bad acquaintance, and introduce her into good society; she would form her opinions and manners. It would be an interesting, and certainly a very kind undertaking, highly becoming her own situation in life, her leisure, and powers. (Chapter 3)

The 'interesting and very kind undertaking' involves preventing Harriet's engagement to Robert Martin (in spite of George Knightley's indignation) and deciding that since she must be the daughter of a gentleman, it is only right that she should marry one.

It is evident that Emma is what we should call a snob, but the word had not yet come into use. Jane Austen's word for her would probably have been 'worldly', and she would have meant by a worldly person one who estimates others by their birth, breeding and wealth—in short, their social status—rather than by their 'minds'. 'Mind', at least as it was used by Jane Austen and Lord Shaftesbury, had a rather different meaning from the modern one. In Chapter 10, Emma remarks of Miss Bates that 'poverty has certainly not contracted her mind', and since it is evident that she considers Miss Bates almost too silly for endurance, she is certainly not referring to her intellect, which indeed Miss Bates is entirely without. What she does possess (as Emma sees, thus showing that she is not altogether worldly) is a large generosity and kindness of nature. It is therefore the quality of a person's nature which Jane Austen means by 'mind'. Emma is well aware of the difference between the implications of mind in this sense and her own worldly standard for the judgment of people, but she does not bring the former critically to bear on the latter, because, at this stage, her social and her personal valuations are kept in separate compartments.

Miss Bates is one of three characters who shed light on Emma's nature by the mixture of obvious contrast with unexpected analogies in their own situations. She comes to Harriet's mind while she ponders the horrid prospect of the unmarried Emma: 'But then, to be an old maid at last, like Miss Bates!' (Chapter 10). Emma has no difficulty in demonstrating that she will never be 'so silly, so satisfied, so smiling, so prosing, so undistinguishing and fastidious, and so apt to tell everything relative to everybody about me' as Miss Bates. But when she gets to giving an account of herself as she expects to be in middle age (in the passage which I have already quoted) she is unable to see that she stands small chance of being as generally beloved as Miss Bates is. Miss Bates is not only perforce unmarried, as Emma proposes to remain, but she is herself aunt of an orphaned niece to whom she is disinterestedly devoted, and who uses her house as a refuge. Miss Bates is indeed a benign bore to everybody, but she interferes with nobody; she has none of Emma's worldliness and no self-regard.

Harriet's limp and drifting mind wanders on to the niece, the second of the parallels to Emma, but at the mention of Jane Fairfax, Emma suddenly becomes bad-tempered:

> 'Do you know Miss Bates's niece? That is, I know you must have seen her a hundred times—but are you acquainted?'
>
> 'Oh, yes; we are always forced to be acquainted whenever she comes to Highbury. By the by, *that* is almost enough to put one out of conceit with a niece. Heaven forbid that I should ever bore people half so much about all the Knightleys together as she does about Jane Fairfax. One is sick of the very name of Jane Fairfax. Every letter from her is read forty times over: her compliments to all friends go round and round again; and if she does send her aunt the pattern of a stomacher, or knit a pair of garters for her grandmother, one hears of nothing else for a month. I wish Jane Fairfax very well; but she bores me to death.'

What is the reason for this disagreeable tone? Emma's remarks are not directly at the expense of Jane herself, but at the fuss made about her; yet they convey an animus against the subject of the fuss. When she arrives in Chapter 20, we find that she is, in person and abilities, at least Emma's equal, and in important respects her superior. She is beautiful, well educated, and musically far more talented. But her circumstances are much inferior. Her mother, like Emma's, is dead, and her father, a penniless army officer, has been killed in action. She has been adopted by her father's commanding officer, Colonel Campbell, who has a daughter of his own. His resources do not suffice for more than to bring her up as a member of his family and equip her with an education sufficient to qualify her as an excellent governess. And since such seems to be her inevitable destiny, she has determined to leave the Campbells at the age of twenty-one—Emma's age—so as to spend her last few months of freedom with her aunt and grandmother.

It seems that Jane is formed to become Emma's intimate friend; she is her only equal personally and of the same sex in Highbury, and materially she is the obvious beneficiary for Emma's abundant philanthropy and wealth. Yet Jane resists Emma's advances with taciturnity and reserve. There are two reasons for this defensiveness. She is the centre of an intrigue which compels her to secrecy, and for other reasons as well she is not a suitable object for Emma's prying patronage. She is thus a tantalizing mystery to Emma, and also a standing reproach to her, both in an obvious way and a subtle one. Her personal superiority together with her material inferiority is an uncomfortable reminder that Emma's self-satisfied independence is due to accidental advantages which she has done nothing to earn. But she is also a reproach in that her friendship can only be had on equal terms, and to meet an equal on equal terms does not suit Emma's complacent nature; such a friendship might expose too much in herself that she is carefully suppressing. When Emma does make advances to Jane in Chapter 20, she is ill-motivated. She knows that Jane has left the Campbells on the engagement of Miss Campbell to a Mr Dixon; the possible implication arouses her taste for intriguing mysteries in other people's lives, and she begins to probe, but she is disappointed:

> [Jane] seemed bent on giving no real insight into Mr Dixon's character, or her own value for his company, or opinion of the suitableness of the match. It was all general approbation and smoothness; nothing delineated or distinguished. It did her no service, however. Her caution was thrown away. Emma saw its artifice, and returned to her first surmises . . . Mr Dixon, perhaps, had been very near changing one friend for the other . . . Emma could not forgive her.

What she cannot forgive, of course (seeing the matter in its worst light), is not that Jane may have been playing games with the affections of two other people, but that she refuses to contribute to Emma's game. But the truth about the natures of the two girls, about their attitudes and their respective situations, is almost the reverse of what is reflected in Emma's mind. It is at least true that Jane is the centre of a mystery, but it is not the one which Emma has gratuitously wished on her. Moreover, Jane has an open, direct nature, and is involved in her mystery involuntarily and reluctantly; it is Emma, whose character seems so open who really relishes deviousness and indirectness, the fabrication of intrigues. Her relish is not due to ill-nature, but to immaturity: other people's lives are, for her at this point, just games, and her own life is no more.

However, Emma at least recognizes that if Jane wishes to resist her patronage, she has the power as well as the right to do so; she remains content with the far easier manipulation of Harriet. But another character enters who feels no such restraints, and she is the third to be erected as a parallel and contrast to Emma herself. This is Augusta Hawkins, whom the vicar, Mr Elton, marries instead of fulfilling Emma's plans which required him to marry Harriet.

Mrs Elton is pretentious, affected, stupid and vulgar. She is fondest of talking about 'My brother Mr Suckling's seat', Maple Grove:

> 'So extremely like Maple Grove! And it is not merely the house—the grounds, I assure you, as far as I could observe, are strikingly like. The laurels at Maple Grove are in the same profusion as here, and stand very much in the same way—just across the lawn; and I had a glimpse of a fine large tree, with a bench round it, which put me so exactly in mind! My brother and sister will be enchanted with this place. People who have extensive grounds are always pleased with anything in the same style.' (Chapter 32)

She is flattering Emma by praising the Woodhouse estate (while indicating that she is well used to such surroundings) because Emma is worth cultivating as the first lady of Highbury—a status in which she intends to supersede her. She likewise assumes intimacy with the 'first gentleman':

> 'And who do you think came in while we were there? . . . Knightley! . . . Knightley himself! . . . I had never seen him before; and of course, as so particular a friend of Mr E's, I had a great curiosity . . . and I must do my *caro sposo* the justice to say that he need not be ashamed of his friend. Knightley's quite the gentleman. . . .'
> (Chapter 32)

Similarly, since it always redounds to prestige to patronize the less fortunate, she becomes a patroness:

> 'My dear Miss Woodhouse, a vast deal may be done by those who dare to act. If *we* set the example, many will follow it as far as they can; though they all have not our situations. *We* have carriages to fetch and convey her home, and *we* live in a style which could not make the addition of Jane Fairfax, at any time, the least inconvenient.' (Chapter 32)

And as being a patroness cannot elevate one in the eyes of others unless they know about it, Mrs Elton advertises her goodness to Jane Fairfax as much as Miss Bates advertises her niece's virtues. It is understandable that Emma should be appalled by Mrs Elton; what she does not see is that Mrs Elton is a caricature of herself.

Both women are perfectly satisfied with themselves, both are arrogant snobs, and neither sees that pride in mere worldly status has a weak foundation. It is true that whereas Emma is justly proud of her own abilities, Mrs Elton has only ostentation of non-existent abilities, but since Emma, as Mr Knightley points out, misuses hers, this comparison is not so greatly to her advantage. The parallel between them is most evident in their common pastime of patronage. Emma has at least the common sense to undertake an interior, but this difference is again not altogether to her advantage, as George Knightley points out:

> '. . . Mrs Elton does not talk *to* Miss Fairfax as she speaks of her . . . you may be sure that Miss Fairfax awes Mrs Elton by her superiority of mind and manner; and that, face to face, Mrs Elton treats her with all the respect which she has a claim to.' (Chapter 33)

He is helping to account for the fact, so strange to Emma, that, far from rebuffing Mrs Elton's advances, Jane responds to them. Jane is in fact lonely, and as Mr Knightley remarks pointedly to Emma, 'she receives attentions from Mrs Elton, which nobody else pays her'. This conversation ends by Emma angering Mr Knightley with the suggestion that he may be unconsciously in love with Jane. He retorts that he has already silenced such an insinuation effectively when it was made by Mr Cole, for 'Cole does not want to be wiser and wittier than his neighbours'. Emma remarks that this is just what Mrs Elton does want to be. But, as several times before, she is making an aspersion which is in fact much truer as a comment about herself. Mrs Elton wants more notice taken of her than of her neighbours, but she does not, in patronizing Jane, try to organize her feelings, which is what Emma does try to do in patronizing Harriet. Mrs Elton is a comic fool which Emma is not, but this only makes Emma's conduct all the worse.

So far we have been tracing Jane Austen's distinctive technique, by which she invites the reader to observe in other characters qualities which both unexpectedly resemble and unexpectedly differ from those in the central one, so that the heroine's moral nature is dramatically displayed for us at levels of which she is not conscious. By this time (Chapter 33) the narrative is well advanced into what we may call its 'second movement' which centres on the third of the 'strangers' to Highbury—Frank Churchill. Before we embark on this new and important actor in the plot, it is as well to summarize the crucial event in the first movement.

The first seventeen chapters concern Emma's abortive scheme to marry Harriet to Mr Elton. With part of her mind, she despises both of them on personal grounds: she knows that the vicar is an empty, socially aspiring young man, and that Harriet's only intrinsic merits are her prettiness and her artless sweetness of nature. But she represses this contempt by concentrating on their social relationship: she has decided that Harriet deserves a superior social status, and Mr Elton has one; this is enough for the game she is playing. When the vicar professes to be enraptured by her portrait of Harriet (which she knows to be mediocre) and rushes off to London to get it framed, she thinks the game is won. And then she is outraged by Mr Elton offering marriage to herself. Her indignation is comic, because she is unable to draw from it the obvious lesson: that in encouraging

Harriet's feelings for the vicar and despising him for herself, she is betraying atrocious arrogance, all the worse because she indignantly attributes to him the very motives which have operated on her on Harriet's behalf: 'Perhaps it was not fair to expect him to feel how very much he was her inferior in talent, and in all the elegancies of mind. The very want of such equality might prevent his perception that in fortune and consequence she was greatly his superior' (Chapter 16).

However, realizing that she may have deeply injured Harriet by giving her false hopes, she does learn at least the danger of trying to direct her affections. But she cannot undo the role she has invented for herself—the conception of herself as mentor which she has implanted in Harriet, nor can she cancel Harriet's elevated expectations. Of these, by poetic justice, Emma is to find herself the astonished victim. As bad is to be Emma's mortifying discovery that she, mistress of the game of intrigue, is to have been a pawn in Frank Churchill's intrigue at the expense of Jane Fairfax.

Frank Churchill

Frank is Mr Weston's son by his first marriage to a Miss Churchill; he has been adopted by his rich and socially arrogant uncle and aunt, and made to take their name. The marriage of his mother and Mr Weston, whose means are moderate, had been a cause of bitterness to the Churchills, but they were childless, so that they became partly reconciled to it by the fact that it provided them with an heir. The result is that Frank has been brought up, like Emma, with easy expectations, but, unlike her, with no close family affections: his tie with his easygoing father has been partly broken, and the Churchills are unlovable. The result, in Jane Austen's conception of the bearing of social upon personal relations, is foreseeable. Frank sees life as a game involving no personal responsibility, and even when he falls in love with Jane Fairfax he is unable to perceive how his behaviour may have consequence for her deepest feelings.

He has met Jane with the Campbells at Weymouth during the autumn previous to the summer in which the events of the novel take place, and become engaged to her. For the Churchills—or rather for Mrs Churchill who dominates her husband—such a union is unthinkable, so that the engagement has to remain secret not only from his adopted parents but also from Highbury, in case rumours of it should escape.

The better to mask his relationship with Jane, Frank behaves as though he is becoming enamoured of Emma, and she, in the enjoyment of the flirtation, responds, though never quite to the point of losing her heart. Thus, just as she had once been sure that she had succeeded in attracting Mr Elton to Harriet Smith, whereas she had unintentionally attracted him to herself, so now she is sure that Frank is drawn to herself, when all the time he is using her as a cover for Jane Fairfax. He relies on her insight (of which she is so proud) to arrive at the truth, but when he gets so far as to hint to her the real state of affairs (Chapter 30), the attempt only confirms her in her misunderstanding.

He secretly buys Jane a piano, leaving her and everybody else in the dark about himself as the giver, and then freely indulges Emma's speculations that it is a gift from the forlorn Mr Dixon, now married to Miss Campbell. He engages Emma as his chief collaborator in arranging a ball, and takes every opportunity of paying open compliments to her, and making discreet but slighting comments on Jane and Jane's appearance. The climax comes on the expedition to Box Hill (Chapter 43). The atmosphere is charged with suppressed, distorted and misunderstood emotion, and Emma reaches her lowest point. Overtly triumphant over Mrs Elton (who had supposed the party to be centred on herself) and flattered by Frank's attentions, she openly flirts with him, and to show off her wit, she is cruelly insulting to Miss Bates.

They are playing a game, in which each person has to say 'one thing very clever . . . or two things moderately clever—or three things very dull indeed'.

'Oh! very well,' exclaimed Miss Bates; 'then I need not be uneasy. 'Three things very dull indeed.' That will just do for me, you know I shall be sure to say three dull things as soon as ever I open my mouth, shan't I?' (Looking round with the most good-humoured dependance on everybody's assent.) 'Do not you all think I shall?'

Emma could not resist.

'Ah! ma'am, but there may be a difficulty. Pardon me—but you will be limited as to number—only three at once.'

Miss Bates, deceived by the mock ceremony of her manner, did not immediately catch her meaning; but when it burst upon her, it could not anger, though a slight blush showed that it could pain her.

'Ah!—well—to be sure. Yes, I see what she means' (turning to Mr Knightley), 'and I will try to hold my tongue. I must make myself very disagreeable, or she would not have said such a thing to an old friend.'

Few other novelists would single out so small an episode, and scarcely any would use it with such telling effect. It epitomizes the theme of the novel: when a game transgresses human feelings, it ceases to be a game and becomes a crime. It is Mr Knightley who makes very clear to Emma that her offence is really a grave one.

Mr Knightley

The code of the society to which they both belong demands courtesy at two levels. The first is superficial merely: the foolish Mrs Elton infringes it when she drops the 'Mr' from George Knightley's name, addressing him merely as 'Knightley'. This is an impertinence, because it assumes familiarity where there is no intimacy, but it reflects mainly on the perpetrator. The deeper level of courtesy exacts the protection of those whose inherent weakness makes them defenceless against the native superiority of those who are socially their equals. Breaches of both laws for the sake of self-display betray vulgarity, but whereas Mrs Elton has merely breached etiquette, Emma's vulgarity is a much deeper moral one.

At Box Hill the division in herself, which has existed all through, reaches its extreme; her games-playing, socially egoistic self prevails, although it is true that she is entirely unconscious of the worst effect she is having: Jane Fairfax is so hurt and confused by her lover's attentions to the wrong woman that she breaks off her engagement. Mr Knightley's rebuke to her marks the turning-point and she begins to make amends, but first she had to realize the great retribution which she has brought on herself. The game she has played with Harriet's heart, framing a real life romance with Harriet as heroine, suddenly takes on a reality which is independent of her, with herself cast for a tragic role in it.

Emma has been led to suspect that Harriet has an inclination for Frank Churchill, because he had rescued her from the gipsies (Chapter 39). In Chapter 40, Harriet speaks mysteriously of a new object of devotion who is immensely her superior, and Emma not unnaturally supposes that it is the gipsy episode which has provoked her feelings—

> 'I am not at all surprised at you, Harriet. The service he rendered you was enough to warm your heart.'
>
> 'Service! oh! it was such an inexpressible obligation! The very recollection of it, and all that I felt at the time, when I saw him coming—his noble look, and my wretchedness before. Such a change! In one moment such a change! From perfect misery to perfect happiness!'

It never occurs to Emma that Harriet, true to her nature, is in fact referring to the ball (Chapter 38) when, flouted by Mr Elton, she would have been left partnerless had it not been for Mr Knightley picking her out. In Chapter 47, Emma, having found out about the engagement between Frank and Jane, now renewed, tries to prepare Harriet for the bad news, and is shocked to find that she is as indifferent to him as Emma is herself. The truth at last dawns on her.

Harriet was standing at one of the windows. Emma turned round to look at her in consternation, and hastily said:

'Have you any idea of Mr Knightley's returning your affection?'

'Yes,' replied Harriet modestly, but not fearfully; 'I must say that I have.'

Emma's eyes were instantly withdrawn; and she sat silently meditating, in a fixed attitude for a few minutes. A few minutes were sufficient for making her acquainted with her own heart. A mind like hers, once opening to suspicion, made rapid progress. She touched she admitted she acknowledged the whole truth Why was it so much worse that Harriet should be in love with Mr Knightley, than with Frank Churchill? Why was the evil so dreadfully increased by Harriet's having some hope of a return? It darted through her, with the speed of an arrow, that Mr Knightley must marry no one but herself!

Her own conduct, as well as her own heart, was before her in the same few minutes. She saw it all with a clearness which had never blessed her before. How improperly had she been acting by Harriet! How inconsiderate, how indelicate, how irrational, how unfeeling had been her conduct! What blindness, what madness, had led her on! It struck her with dreadful force, and she was ready to give it every bad name in the world.

At last she has done with games: she realizes that not only has she been a pawn in Frank Churchill's, but has become one in her own.

But what Harriet hopes are signs of Mr Knightley's attraction to her are in fact merely his characteristic kindness to one whom he considers has been misused. Explanation between him and Emma comes in Chapter 49, and is heralded by a symbolic change in physical tone induced by the weather:

The weather continued much the same all the following morning; and the same loneliness, and the same melancholy, seemed to reign at Hartfield—but in the afternoon it cleared; the wind changed into a softer quarter; the clouds were carried off; the sun appeared; it was summer again. With all the eagerness which such a transition gives, Emma resolved to be out of doors as soon as possible. Never had the exquisite sight, smell, sensation of nature, tranquil, warm, and brilliant after a storm, been more attractive to her. She longed for the serenity they might gradually introduce; and on Mr Perry's coming in soon after dinner, with a disengaged hour to give to her father, she lost no time in hurrying into the shrubbery. There, with spirits freshened, and thoughts a little relieved, she had taken a few turns, when she saw Mr Knightley passing through the garden door, and coming towards her.

From the beginning he has represented honest, disinterested insight and concern, and it is true that he has the rather unpopular characteristic of being always right—in direct contrast to Emma who has been always wrong. He has taken the true measure of Harriet Smith, of both the Eltons, of Jane Fairfax, and of Frank Churchill in turn; most of all, he has taken the true measure of Emma herself. Yet he is never complacently and unctuously right; he is humble in his own assessment of Emma's feelings towards him, and he has an engaging directness of speech which always displays his real state of mind even when a superficial and mistaken notion of politeness would seem to dictate concealment of it. It is, for instance, worth considering the brusqueness of his tone when he converses from horseback with Miss Bates through the open window at the end of Chapter 28—a masterpiece of natural dialogue: whereas Emma's wounding witticism is conveyed with elegantly turned phrase, his irritability at Miss Bates's chatter is transmitted with no effect of unkindness and causes her no offence.

More than any other male character in Jane Austen's novels, Mr Knightley seems to stand for an ideal in her conception of a civilized man of the class to which she belonged: practical but with deep feeling, robust but delicate in perception, energetically direct but with strong powers of restraint; above all, strongly traditional in his sense of what is owing to the obligations of his status and to people, and in the truthfulness of response which he believes due to both. In a previous section, I suggested that he represented for Jane Austen the values of Dr Johnson (without Johnson's eccentricities, however), and it is strange how seldom it has been perceived that such strength, delicacy and balanced integrity are the essentials she saw in that part of the civilization of her day that she admired. He is opposed to Frank Churchill, who indeed characterizes the risks she saw her civilization undergoing, and this opposition is evident in his remarks on Frank's explanatory letter in Chapter 51:

'Very bad—though it might have been worse. Playing a most dangerous game. Too much indebted to the event for his acquittal. No judge of his own manners by you. Always deceived in fact by his own wishes, and regardless of little besides his own convenience. Fancying you to have fathomed his secret! Natural enough!—his own mind full of intrigue, that he should suspect it in others. Mystery; finesse—how they pervert the understanding! My Emma, does not everything serve to prove more and more the beauty of truth and sincerity in all our dealings with each other?'

Perhaps he is rather too strict, too straightforward. His concluding sentence should be put beside Jane Austen's own, epigraph to this section, but now in the light of the whole novel it is relevant to continue it:

> Seldom, very seldom, does complete truth belong to any human disclosure; seldom can it happen that something is not a little disguised, or a little mistaken; but where, as in this case, though the conduct is mistaken, the feelings are not, it may not be very material. Mr Knightley could not impute to Emma a more relenting heart than she possessed, or a heart more disposed to accept of his.

Jane Austen seems to be saying that if 'the beauty of truth and sincerity in all our dealings with each other' is too abstracted from the facts of human motivation for ordinary relationships, they can become a reality in the essence of a relationship when in an act of mutual recognition two people spontaneously relinquish their motives for self-deception. It is not so much the achievement of a balance between feeling and judgment, as an acknowledgement that the distinction between them has become irrelevant, since both have come to rest in their destination.

13 Jane Austen's Place in English Fiction

> That young lady had a talent for describing the involvement and feelings and characters of ordinary life which is to me the most wonderful I ever met with. The Big Bow-wow strain I can do myself like any now going, but the exquisite touch which renders ordinary commonplace things and characters interesting from the truth of the description and the sentiment is denied me. What a pity such a gifted creature died so early!
>
> WALTER SCOTT: Journal, 14 March 1826

Scott was the earliest of the distinguished critical admirers of Jane Austen. The first critique of her work by an eminent hand was his review of *Emma*, into which he incorporated a survey of her other work, though he omitted *Mansfield Park*. Yet this generally admiring account includes the following paragraph:

> Upon the whole, the turn of this author's novels bears the same relation to that of the sentimental and romantic cast, that corn-fields and cottages and meadows bear to the highly adorned grounds of a show mansion, or the rugged sublimities of a mountain landscape. It is neither so captivating as the one, nor so grand as the other, but it affords to those who frequent it a pleasure nearly allied with their own social habits; and what is of some importance, the youthful wanderer may return from his promenade to the ordinary business of life, without any chance of having his head turned by the recollection of the scene through which he has been wandering.

This is a curiously betraying passage. On the one hand, Scott is defining Jane Austen's limitations (she does not admit what is 'grand' into her fictions), but on the other hand he associates the grand with what is theatrical and misleading: the 'show mansion' and the 'chance of having his head turned'. It is worth quoting again, beside this paragraph of Scott's, the one from Gilpin's 'On picturesque travel':

> Some artists, when they give the imagination play, let it loose among uncommon scenes—such as perhaps never existed: whereas the nearer they approach the simple standard of nature in its more

Steventon Parsonage

beautiful forms, the more admirable their fictions appear. It is thus in writing romances. The correct taste cannot bear those unnatural situations in which heroes and heroines are often placed, whereas a story *naturally* and of course affectingly told, either with pen or pencil, though known to be a fiction, is considered as a transcript from nature; and takes possession of the heart. The *marvellous* disgusts the sober imagination; which is gratified only with the pure characters of the natural.

Gilpin here faces without Scott's ambiguity the danger of the concept of 'grandeur' in art, and he also states that there is no necessary relationship between the familiarity of a scene and the depth of its appeal. However, his use of the now dated term 'affectingly told' does not adequately convey what for us is the true force of such an art as Jane Austen's. It suggests an appeal to what Gilpin would probably have called 'the sentiments', a word which conveyed to his contemporaries something richer than it conveys to us, but still would not be sufficient to counterbalance the lack in Jane Austen of an equivalence to Scott's 'rugged sublimities of a mountain landscape'. This amounts to saying that Jane Austen does not communicate 'the passions'.

This criticism was first made forcibly by Charlotte Brontë, who wrote:

The Passions are perfectly unknown to her; even to the Feelings she vouchsafes no more than an occasional graceful but distant recognition; too frequent converse with them would but ruffle the elegance of her progress. Her business is not half so much with the human heart as with the human eyes, mouth, hands and feet: what sees keenly, speaks aptly, moves flexibly, it suits her to study, but what throbs fast and full, though hidden, what the blood rushes through, what is the unseen seat of Life, and the sentient target of death—*this* Miss Austen ignores; she no more, with her mind's eye, beholds the heart of her race than each man, with bodily vision, sees the heart in his heaving breast.

It would be possible to answer this by suggesting that it really answers itself. Just as the physical eye infers the existence of the heart, so the mind's eye has to infer the passions of people whose outward behaviour is socially normal; and it is precisely a talent for observation which Charlotte Brontë acknowledges Jane Austen to possess. Charlotte Brontë's real criticism, however, is perhaps that Jane Austen does not identify with her characters as she identified with her own, thus making inference unnecessary to the reader because the passions are communicated directly to him. If this is her real point, then it seems that we are merely faced with two different kinds of novelist, neither of whom is necessarily better than the other: in Jane Austen, the social surface is perfect, but the passions are only implied; in Charlotte Brontë the surface is often crude or sketchy, but the passions have the force of immediacy. Still, there may be good reasons for preferring the second kind of novelist (with or without Charlotte Brontë's defects), and to understand what these reasons might be, we need to pass on to a basically similar, though profounder and far more virulent comment by D. H. Lawrence in his essay *A Propos of Lady Chatterley's Lover* (1929):

> This, again, is the tragedy of social life today. In the old England, the curious blood-connection held the classes together. The squires might be arrogant, violent, bullying and unjust, yet in some ways they were *at one* with the people, part of the same blood-stream. We feel it in Defoe or Fielding. And then, in the mean Jane Austen, it is gone. Already this old maid typifies 'personality' instead of character, the sharp knowing in apartness instead of knowing in togetherness, and she is, to my feeling, thoroughly unpleasant, English in the bad, mean, snobbish sense of the word, just as Fielding is English in the good generous sense.

Lawrence is concerned with human relationships whereas Charlotte Brontë does not mention them, but the passages are alike in two respects. Both writers describe living in terms of the unseen—'what the blood rushes through' and the 'blood connection'; both also see in Jane Austen an 'apartness': Lawrence contrasting her concern for 'personality' (from the Latin *persona*—a mask) with 'character', and Charlotte Brontë her acute observation of social behaviour with the life of the human heart. In a letter to Edward Garnett (June 1914) Lawrence speaks of abandoning what he calls the 'social ego' for the sake of exploring what underlies it.

It is not important to defend Jane Austen by meeting these criticisms head on; it is more enlightening to try to understand why they were made. We can easily guess some of the less interesting motives: for instance, one may suppose that Lawrence was smarting against the banning of his novel in accordance with a taste which, he may have thought, conformed to some concept of Jane Austen's gentility. But Lawrence's language is not just hysterical rage, and Charlotte Brontë's does not issue merely from the obtuseness of a socially unsophisticated woman. Their disagreement with Jane Austen is a genuine one, worth examining if we are to understand where she stands in the English tradition.

In all imaginative literature of every period, the individual has been set in polar opposition to some concept of an all-embracing power which limits and defines him, and sometimes constitutes his antagonist, but always binds him into community with other individuals. The individual is the microcosm, in more or less uneasy relationship with the macrocosm, and through that with his fellow individuals. This macrocosm might be designated the gods, or God, or Nature, or sometimes even erotic love. Such ideas imply a religious vision, and they operated so long as a fundamentally religious notion of the world prevailed in all ranks of society, so that mere social status, however imposing or degraded, was not felt to include the whole significance of man. But in the second half of the seventeenth century a number of influences eroded this spiritual interpretation of the world; they included the rise to power of the middle classes and the scepticism of practical thinkers who relied on new-found scientific uses of the reason which superseded the imaginative responses. This new practical thinking shortened the individual's perspectives in respect to the forces with which he had to contend. It was still rare for thinking men to deny the existence of ultimate realities, but in practice they concerned themselves more with those relatively powerful forces which immediately affected the conduct of their lives. These were above all social, and focused on the most central of all our social institutions—marriage and the family. This was why the new form of the novel arose and was so popular. Novels might be despised but they were read widely because they dealt with the kind of reality in which the reading public was most interested.

On the other hand the reading public, especially perhaps the middle-class young woman, was partly resistant to the recognition of themselves as, foremost, social animals. Their attitude to society was ambivalent. Any society must be to some extent constraining, arbitrary, hypocritical and unjust, promoting some who are unworthy and victimizing others who deserve better. Hence there was a strong escapist element in most even of the best eighteenth-century novels. If the hero or heroine had experiences denied to the ordinary man or woman, or achieved promise of lasting happiness beyond earthly probability, or was endowed with qualities beyond any normal endowment but not beyond the reader's wishfulness, then the reader was gratified by a liberation through fantasy although it was unavailable to him in actuality. But he might feel a more developed kind of ambivalence. He might believe that at its best his society represented the highest standards of civilization yet embodied, but that, in practice, it fell far below the standards it professed. Then novels might satisfy him by exhibiting ideal exemplars (like Richardson's *Sir Charles Grandison*) or (like those of Fielding) that they exposed social falsification of what is best in human nature. In briefest terms, one may say that the eighteenth-century reader felt that, at worst, society was a necessary evil, but that at best it represented (what the Victorian critic Matthew Arnold thought the state should be) 'the best self' of men and women of his kind. In either case, bad or good, society was the inescapable element in which the individual had to live, like the bird in the air or the fish in the water.

By the Victorian period, opening some twenty years after Jane Austen's death, much in attitudes to society had changed. In consequence of the Industrial Revolution, men could enrich themselves to an extent and with a speed that was unprecedented, but the Victorians were painfully aware that the proletariat of the new industrial towns neither shared this prosperity nor were inclined to remain passive in their deprivation, as the labouring classes in the eighteenth century had been. Then, the Romantics' expounding of faith in the feelings often resulted in personal instability and frustration, so that the individual was aware of a turbulence within himself matching the social turbulence he saw without. There was much less agreement among educated people about what their society represented and ought to represent: the elation and optimism of Macaulay confronted the bitter forebodings of Matthew Arnold. Phrases like 'the Hidden Soul' (E. S. Dallas) and 'the Buried Self' (Arnold) showed the growth of the belief that real living went on below the social surface where, as Tennyson wrote in *Locksley Hall*, 'the individual withers'. Novels like those of the Brontë sisters and of the later Dickens contained poetic and symbolic elements for which ordinary social converse was not any longer a natural medium. That society was no longer the natural element for the fully conscious human being began in fact to be a theme for the imaginative writer to ponder, and gives novelists at the turn into the twentieth century—Hardy, James, Conrad—a new sombreness. Part of this scepticism shows itself in a new attitude to social class. In the eighteenth and nineteenth centuries, social class was a kind of common denominator for understanding between authors and readers: a character's social class might not be the most important aspect of him, but at least it could be assumed that he had one, and it was embracing enough as a characteristic of his personality to serve as a means of introducing him. D. H. Lawrence—the first major English novelist to have had a genuinely working-class background—was also the first to show how social class no longer sufficed to express even a character's surface. Yet no sane man could doubt that human beings had to live in relationship; relationship must, however, arise from deeper sources of life than society could offer. Hence Lawrence's insistence on the 'blood connection'.

Writing in the first two decades of the nineteenth century, Jane Austen appears historically, both in her social attitudes and formally in her art, as a kind of connecting link or hinge. Her attitude to society was still an eighteenth-century one: she assumed a permanence in its order and in the values of that order. But in her attitude to the individual she looks forward to the later nineteenth century: not only is the individual ensconced within a distinctive social setting, but he or she is faced with decisions that are primarily personal, although they have an unavoidable social bearing.

Her sense of social identity was much clearer than that of earlier novelists had been. She abandoned the romantic licences, in characterization and incident, which had enabled her predecessors to loosen the close tie between the character and his society, and accepted that the immediate day-to-day environment was inescapably the theatre in which the character's fate had to be decided. At the same time, the conflict between the heroine and her environment is reflected in her mental state, so that she has to resolve inwardly a tangle in which egoistic revolt is confused with false motives for conformity, sometimes the one, sometimes the other being uppermost. It follows that the heroines have an interior life which relates closely to the exterior one, so that they are closer to normal beings living in normal circumstances than earlier heroes and heroines had been. But Jane Austen differs from many later novelists in her insistence that the heroine can never step apart from her society in her adventure of discovery; any attempt to pursue the 'passions' as entities somehow unrelated to social living is open to suspicion—not of individualism but of egoism—of ulterior motives or plain exhibitionistic folly, or a mixture of these.

However, when we think of Jane Austen's treatment of character-in-society, it is important to recognize the extent to which her novels underwent development and enrichment of technique. The most obvious feature of this advance is the greater substance of the settings in the last three novels. In *Pride and Prejudice*, for instance, Meryton is merely the neighbouring town with no particular significance of its own as environment of the characters, but in *Emma* Highbury has a real social identity and Emma's position in it has much to do with the nature of her predicament, and her relationship to the other characters (Mr Knightley, Mr Weston, the Eltons, Mrs Bates, Jane Fairfax) is influenced by their own relationship to the place. Similarly, in *Pride and Prejudice* the houses—Longbourn, Netherfield, Rosings, Pemberley—matter as suitable backgrounds for the characters who inhabit them, but in *Mansfield Park* the house is much more than merely that: it represents a system of values amounting to a civilization in itself, contrasting with the more liberal but also more unstable values of the Grantleys and of the Crawfords, with their London roots, in the neighbouring vicarage, and still more with those of the Prices in chaotic Portsmouth. Thus the heroines of *Mansfield Park* and *Emma* do not merely contend with other individuals representing social attitudes but also with climates of feeling and opinion: in the former, the pressure of this climate is almost enough to frustrate in Fanny Price any growth of independent selfhood, although it also nourishes and sustains in her values that she can trust; in the latter, Emma's privileged position in her society nearly dooms her by inflating her egoism. In both novels we live in the heroine's mind as we read, but we experience the minds of Fanny and Emma more fully than we do those of

Elizabeth Bennet or the Dashwood girls in *Sense and Sensibility*, in the same way as we know people in real life much better for a fuller knowledge of the circumstances that have shaped them.

Naturally, one sees this difference most clearly in the two posthumously published novels, *Northanger Abbey* and *Persuasion*, the earliest written and the latest, and some comparison of these two is the more inviting since both are partly set in the fashionable city of Bath. In the former, the heroine enters the city in the company of the placid, empty-minded Mrs Allen, wholly preoccupied with her belongings:

> Nothing more alarming occurred than a fear, on Mrs Allen's side, of having once left her clogs behind her at an inn, and that fortunately proved to be groundless.
>
> They arrived at Bath. Catherine was all eager delight; her eyes were here, there, everywhere, as they approached its fine and striking environs, and afterwards drove through those streets which conducted them to the hotel. She was come to be happy, and she felt happy already.
>
> They were soon settled in comfortable lodgings in Pulteney Street. (Chapter 2)

In *Persuasion*, the much older heroine, Anne Elliot, is accompanied by her friend the sophisticated Lady Russell:

> Everybody has their taste in noises as well as in other matters; and sounds are quite innoxious or most distressing, by their sort rather than their quantity. When Lady Russell, not long afterwards, was entering Bath, on a wet afternoon, and driving through the long course of streets from the Old Bridge to Camden Place, amidst the dash of other carriages, the heavy rumble of carts and drays, the bawling of newsmen, muffin-men, and milkmen, and the ceaseless clink of pattens, she made no complaint. No, these were noises which belonged to the winter pleasures; her spirits rose under their influence; and, like Mrs Musgrove, she was feeling, though not saying, that after being long in the country nothing could be so good for her as a little quiet cheerfulness.
>
> Anne did not share these feelings. She persisted in a very determined, though very silent, disinclination for Bath; caught the first dim view of the extensive buildings, smoking in rain, without any wish of seeing them better; felt their progress through the streets to be, however disagreeable, yet too rapid; for who would be glad to see her when she arrived? (Chapter 14)

Both passages are well suited to the purposes of the very different stories of the very different heroines, but the difference is richer than just that of character. In neither do the older and younger woman feel the need to communicate, but significantly in the second passage the novelist points to the silence between them—'she was feeling, though not saying', 'a very determined, though very silent, disinclination'—whereas in the first we take it for granted. We assume, in *Northanger Abbey*, that Mrs Allen notices nothing but vaguely anticipates a pleasant time, whereas we are told that Catherine responds excitedly to everything, reflecting on nothing because it is all new; they are silently comfortable with each other because they are without worries and share expectations of pleasure, though of a different sort. In *Persuasion*, although the relationship is long-standing and deep, each is silent because each is in a state of mind quite apart from the other's: Lady Russell feels a refreshment of spirit which is sufficient to itself and requires no sharing, whereas Anne is suffering a depression of spirit which is incommunicable even to her old friend. We are made to feel the nature of place much more concretely in the *Persuasion* passage, not because it is distinguished as one town and not another—they might as well have been entering Cheltenham or Brighton—but because the novelist is concerned to show how differently the impact of any environment affects quite different states of mind. Moreover, what differentiates Anne from her companion in this episode marks her difference from those about her throughout the novel until she is reunited with her lost lover, Captain Wentworth. This is her apartness.

The sense of being and feeling 'apart' from others characterizes in one way all Jane Austen's heroines, because the reader is made to experience the story through the heroine's point of view, but it is true in a different sense for Anne in *Persuasion*, because the novel begins when, to appearance, her story has finished. We learn that alone of her family she resembles her mother, and that her mother has died; that she shares nothing with her father and her two sisters in common interests or mutual sympathy, and is appreciated only by Lady Russell, whose prudent counsel has nonetheless prevented her marrying the only man she has loved and who has loved her in return. She has thus lost one prospect of happiness and has no other in a world from which she is alienated. And yet Anne Elliot is not at all a dismal character; the reader acquires affection and respect for her because, instead of understandably withdrawing into a state of resentfulness and self-pity (which in fact characterize her not very happily married sister Mary) she continues to serve the relationships she has inherited as best she can, though without appreciation and often with hidden pain. The pain becomes much more acute when Captain Wentworth returns from the wars—now prosperous and with good status, thus proving that Lady Russell's prudential counsels were mistaken—and she has to watch what seems to be his progressive attraction to Mary's sister-in-law, Louisa Musgrove. She has, it seems, by obedience to her only friend's worldly advice, condemned herself to a lifetime of serving others without reward, and watching their self-willed error without any hope of attention to her warnings and advice, and moreover to be made witness to the confirmation of the loss of her lover by his own change of heart.

Of course Anne might have sunk into resigned indifference to her fate, but Wentworth's return keeps her in involuntary tensions with what happens in her surroundings. It is this sense of the paradoxical fusion of apartness with involvement which gives the reader a sense of the substantiality of the heroine's environment in *Persuasion*. For instance, in *Northanger Abbey* we learn very little about the character of Bath society, and this is natural because its heroine is too inexperienced to make judgments upon it, and she has no motive for attempting them; she learns through the individuals she meets, and acquires understanding of the difference between fashion-seeking nonentities like the Thorpes and the intelligent, disillusioned scepticism of Henry Tilney, but this is all. But in *Persuasion*, through Anne's eyes, we acquire the elements of a social geography of the place. She already knows her father's infatuation with appearances, especially his own, but she has to observe the absurdity of his cultivation of the Dalrymples merely because they have even greater prestige of rank, and she has to feel the extreme of his superciliousness to his social inferiors in his opinion that to be surnamed Smith and to live in Westgate Buildings is virtually not to exist at all. She sees the gradual corrosion of Mrs Clay's parasitry on her father and her sister Elizabeth, and learns the beguiling machinations of Mr Elliot to ensure his inheritance of her father's title. We are shown Austenian gentry at their worst —bigoted, narrow, arrogant, and useless: no country gentleman in the previous novels has quite as much self-conceit and obliviousness to responsibilities as Sir Walter does, and no intriguer has been quite so skilfully devious for petty ends as Mr Elliot is. However, the most striking innovation is the contrast provided by a new constituent in this society: the naval officers and their ladies, who tolerate but implicitly despise the values of the established society.

The naval contingent have achieved repute not from inherited status but from the wars. They have no regard for appearances except as they correspond to truth: Admiral Croft's ridicule of the picture in the printshop (Chapter 18) of a ship that could not possibly sail—'I would not venture over a horsepond in it'—is not just the ignorance of an old philistine who does not understand art but the attitude of a professional who believes that artists too should be professionals and respect the criteria of reality. Whereas for a landowner of Sir Walter's kind reality is how to use his material resources to sustain his vanity, for the sailors and their wives it is how to survive dangers and hardships without evasion of duty. This does not make them intrinsically superior in self-knowledge and maturity of feeling: Captain Harville is duly shocked in Chapter 23 at his friend Benwick's ingenuous volatility of feeling when he transfers the gift of a portrait of himself from his former fiancée, now dead, to Louisa, his new beloved. But the conversation that follows (overheard by Wentworth) has a seriousness and sincerity unimaginable in Anne's own circle. It is not only that Harville takes feelings seriously but that he, like his colleagues, is able to see Anne as a woman of insight and truthfulness, unlike her own family and friends, with the partial exception of Lady Russell.

The event which is the turning-point in the story—Louisa Musgrove's fall on the Cobb at Lyme Regis—is another innovation in *Persuasion*. It has often been noticed as the only overtly dramatic incident in all the six novels; even the elopement of Lydia and Wickham in *Pride and Prejudice* occurs off-stage. A common remark is that Louisa's fall is the most that Jane Austen could manage in direct drama, but it illustrates a virtue of her realism and not a weakness in her imagination: in secure circumstances of life it is precisely such an episode—a flighty young girl taking a foolish risk—that does bring tragedy. Structurally, the significance of the incident is twofold. In the first place, the risk that Louisa takes of jumping into Wentworth's arms before he is ready for her is symbolic of the risk that Anne did not take when she refused Wentworth's first offer; in Chapter 23 she tells him that she still believes that she had been right to have made this refusal. Secondly, she is able to show the real strength of her character for the first time; it is she who keeps her head and sees what needs to be done, while the two other women respectively faint and scream hysterically, and the men are shocked into immobility. It is a suitable crisis for the action of the novel because the two men of action on the scene— Benwick and Wentworth—are unequipped to meet the emergency, unexpected as it is in the sheltered society to which they have returned, where life has seemed to be all games and display, and the real action lies hidden. They are, however, qualified to see how, imprisoned though she is by her circumstances (just as at this moment she is restricted by the need to support Louisa's fainting sister), she is potentially the woman with the virtues which their profession enables them to respect. Because he is able to see these virtues, Wentworth is now able to release her from the constraints which have hitherto effaced her. But of course the release does not come easily. Mr Elliot's cultivation of Anne for his own purposes, and Wentworth's awareness that he is himself, not only once rejected by her, but also an outsider to her society, very nearly frustrates Anne's final hopes; it is only by the indirect and unconscious intervention of Harville by their dialogue in Chapter 23 that she is at the last moment saved.

It is well known that this final episode was a rewriting after a first draft which made the reconciliation due to a less plausible accident. Jane Austen had faced herself with an almost insuperable problem. The opportunities for intelligent girls of her class and time to achieve freedom and fulfilment were at best rare and easily frustrated, and all her novels concern this predicament, but in *Persuasion* the unlikely opportunity had already been refused. The refusal enabled the novelist to build up in her heroine the image of a mature woman facing the prospect of effacement and deprivation for the rest of her life, and the success of the novel is due to making the reader feel this negative predicament positively, not merely through the novelist's mind but through that of Anne Elliot herself. This makes *Persuasion* the most mature of her novels and therefore in one way a fitting conclusion to Jane Austen's work.

However, it is also well known that, when she had completed *Persuasion* as we know it, not long before her death, she set it aside as not yet ready for publication. It is of course hopeless to speculate what changes she might have made, but just as the novel has new strengths, so it also has weaknesses which are unprecedented in her work: the dulness of Mrs Smith who is little more than a cog in the plot mechanism; a failure to present Mr Elliot's character with a force to match his importance in the plot. They are both in themselves new departures of character creation, and if we read *Persuasion* together with her last fragment, *Sanditon*, we may reasonably suppose that she had reached a point in her career when she felt the need to assimilate a new social factor into her fiction.

In one word, the new factor which later novelists had to take into account is—change. In each of the six novels, it is the established order which is in the foreground; the possibilities of change and decay are within or imminent, rather than actual. That this way of seeing her environment was not necessarily inherent in Jane Austen, but imposed on her by the society she knew, can be illustrated by reference to *Sanditon*. It was known under this title though Austen family tradition records that she intended to call it *The Brothers*.

Unlike the settings of the other novels, Sanditon is not a prosperous, long-established place; it is a fishing village being puffed into a seaside resort by the speculative enterprise of the local squire, Mr Parker, in collaboration with a mean, mercenary, distinctly spurious local 'great lady', Lady Denham. Mr Parker is an ingenuous, energetic, extremely optimistic projector, whose publicity has much of the ring of modern advertising:

> The Sea air & Sea Bathing together were nearly infallible, one or other of them being a match for every Disorder, of the Stomach, the lungs or the Blood; They were anti-spasmodic, anti-pulmonary, anti-septic, anti-bilious & anti-rheumatic. Nobody could catch cold by the Sea, Nobody wanted Appetite by the Sea, Nobody wanted Spirits, Nobody wanted Strength.—They were healing, softing, relaxing—fortifying & bracing—seemingly just as was wanted—sometimes one, sometimes the other.—If the Sea breeze foiled, the Sea Bath was the certain corrective; —& where Bathing

disagreed, the Sea Breeze was evidently designed by Nature for the cure.

Mr Parker is not interested in the continuance of what is established—'not that he had any personal concern for the Village itself; for considering it too remote from the Beach, he had done nothing there'—and for him civilization, like ours, is the evidence of new construction and consumer goods:

> Civilization, Civilization indeed!—cried Mr P—, delighted—. Look my dear Mary Look at William Heeley's windows.—Blue Shoes, & nankin Boots!—Who wd have expected such a sight at a Shoemaker's in old Sanditon!—This is new within the Month. There was no blue Shoe when we passed this way a month ago.—Glorious indeed!—Well, I think I *have* done something in my Day.—Now, for our Hill, our health-breathing Hill.—

He has abandoned his own self-providing estate, neatly settled in the contours of the valley, and has persuaded himself that it is better to live in an exposed situation unrelated to the structure of the landscape or to any needs of living beyond the attraction of a seasonal population of visitors. From being a producer he has become a speculator, dependent on producers. All the same, the new Sanditon, as a setting has excitement and movement, something of the stimulation of constant change which is infectious in such Victorian novels as *Dombey and Son*:

> Trafalgar House, on the most elevated spot on the Down was a light elegant Building, standing in a small Lawn with a very young plantation round it, about an hundred yards from the brow of a steep, but not very lofty Cliff—and the nearest to it, of every Building, except the Terrace, with a broad walk in front, aspiring to be the Mall of the Place. In this row were the best Milliner's shop & the Library—a little detached from it, the Hotel & Billiard Room—Here began the Descent to the Beach, & to the Bathing Machines—& this was therefore the favourite spot for Beauty & Fashion.—At Trafalgar House, rising a little distance behind the Terrace, the Travellers were safely set down, & all was Happiness & Joy between Papa & Mama & their Children; while Charlotte having received possession of her apartment, found amusement enough in standing at her ample Venetian window, & looking over the miscellaneous foreground of unfinished Buildings, waving Linen, & tops of Houses, to the Sea, dancing & sparkling in Sunshine & Freshness.

The house in College Street, Winchester, in which Jane Austen died after she had moved to Winchester to be near her physician in her last illness

It is worth remembering that Jane Austen died at forty-two, at the height of her powers. It is painful to have missed what she might have done with such a place and the mixed society which it attracted. What we have is enough to show that she may have been about to move into a new phase—one in which changefulness would have been in the foreground instead of present by implication only. She might, in fact, have lived to become our first great Victorian novelist.

Part Four
Reference Section

Bibliography

The most authoritative text is the Oxford edition edited with annotations by R. W. Chapman. Each volume has appendices relevant to all the novels; I cite some of the most useful of these.

I. *Sense and Sensibility*, 1811
Notes on Jane Austen's language.

II. *Pride and Prejudice*, 1813
Appendices on indebtedness to Fanny Burney's *Cecilia*, and on modes of address in the novels.

III. *Mansfield Park*, 1814
This volume includes Kotzebue's play *Lovers' Vows*, translated by Mrs Inchbald; this is important for understanding certain episodes in the story. Appendices on 'Improvements' and on Carriages and Travel.

IV. *Emma*, 1816
Appendices on Manners (including recreations such as dancing), and on Jane Austen's punctuation.

V. *Northanger Abbey;*
Persuasion, 1818
Including notes on and excerpts from Mrs Radcliffe's *The Mysteries of Udolpho*. Also a list of literary allusions in the novels and letters. Includes 'Biographical Notice' by H. T. Austen.

VI. *Minor Works*
This volume includes not only the Juvenilia but works of Jane Austen's adult years left in manuscript at her death: *The Watsons; Lady Susan; Sanditon*.

VII. Southam, B. *Jane Austen's 'Sir Charles Grandison'*, Clarendon Press, 1980. This is a dramatic sketch formerly thought to be by Jane Austen's niece Anna, but now authenticated as her own, possibly written for her niece's entertainment.

Jane Austen's Letters to her sister Cassandra and others edited by R. W. Chapman, Oxford University Press, 1952.
This is the most complete edition, from which a selection has been made by the editor for the World's Classics.

AUSTEN, HENRY THOMAS. 'Biographical Notice of the Author' prefixed to the first edition of *Northanger Abbey* and *Persuasion* and included in vol. V of the Oxford edition mentioned above.

AUSTEN-LEIGH, J. E.   *A Memoir of Jane Austen* (1871), Oxford University Press, 1926, edited by R. W. Chapman.

CHAPMAN, R. W.   *Jane Austen—Facts and Problems*, Oxford University Press, 1948.
Clark Lectures. A useful, brief reference work.

PINION, F. B.   *A Jane Austen Companion*, Macmillan, 1973.
A comprehensive reference book, with extensive information about the novels.

CRAIK, W. A.   *Jane Austen in her Time*, Nelson, 1969.

JENKINS, ELIZABETH.   *Jane Austen, a Biography*, Macdonald (revised edition, 1956.)
The most up-to-date extended biography.

LASKI, MARGHANITA.   *Jane Austen and her World*, Thames and Hudson, 1969.
A very well-illustrated short life, with well-chosen information.

Criticism

Nineteenth century

SOUTHAM, B. C., ed,   *Jane Austen: the Critical Heritage*, Routledge, 1968.
A collection of critical essays, references and comments from Jane Austen's lifetime until 1870.

Twentieth century
Critics in the last half century have explored Jane Austen's work with much greater thoroughness than those of the preceding hundred years. The following is a selection of some of the best-known studies:

LASCELLES, MARY.   *Jane Austen and Her Art*, Oxford University Press, 1939.

WRIGHT, ANDREW H.   *Jane Austen's Novels: A Study in Structure*, Chatto & Windus, 1961.

CRAIK, W. A.   *Jane Austen: the Six Novels*, Methuen, 1965.

LITZ, A. W.   *Jane Austen: a Study in her Literary Development*, Chatto & Windus, 1953, (second edition, 1961).

HARDY, BARBARA.   *A Reading of Jane Austen*, Peter Owen, 1975.

CECIL, DAVID.   *A Portrait of Jane Austen*, Constable, 1978.

There have also been collections of critical essays each including work by various hands:

WATT, IAN, ed.   *Jane Austen: a Collection of Critical Essays*, Prentice-Hall, 1963.

SOUTHAM, B. C., ed.   *Critical Essays on Jane Austen*, Routledge, 1968.

O'NEILL, J., ed. *Critics on Jane Austen*, Allen & Unwin (Readings in
    Literary Criticism), 1970.
MONAGHAN, DAVID, ed. *Jane Austen in a Social Context*, Macmillan,
    1982.

The following combine assessment of Jane Austen's art with an investigation of her social attitudes:

HARDING, D. W.   'Regulated hatred: an aspect of the work of Jane
    Austen', in Ian Watt's collection above, 1963.
MUDRICK, MARVIN. *Jane Austen: Irony as Defense and Discovery*, Princeton
    University Press, 1952.
DUCKWORTH, A. M.   *The Improvement of the Estate: a Study of Jane
    Austen's Novels*, Johns Hopkins Press, 1971.
DEVLIN, D. D.   *Jane Austen and Education*, Macmillan, 1975.
BUTLER, MARILYN.   *Jane Austen and the War of Ideas*, Clarendon Press,
    1975.
BROWN, JULIA PREWITT.   *Jane Austen's Novels: Social Change and Literary
    Form*, Harvard University Press, 1979.
ROBERTS, WARREN.   *Jane Austen and the French Revolution*, Macmillan,
    1979.
KIRKHAM, MARGARET.   *Jane Austen: Feminism and Fiction*, Harvester
    Press, 1983.

Specialized studies:

BABB, H. S.   *Jane Austen's Novels: the Fabric of Dialogue*, Ohio University
    Press, 1962.
SOUTHAM, B. C.   *Jane Austen's Literary Manuscripts*, Oxford University
    Press (Oxford English Monographs), 1964.
    A study of those of her novels, from *Love and Freindship* to
    Sanditon, not included in the six novels.
BRADBROOK, F. W.   *Jane Austen and Her Predecessors*, Cambridge
    University Press, 1966.
    A useful study of the eighteenth-century literary background to
    Jane Austen's work.
LEAVIS, Q. D.   *A Critical Theory of Jane Austen's Writings*, Cambridge
    University Press, 1963. Essays reprinted from *Scrutiny* Vol. X,
    1941; also in *A Selection from Scrutiny*, Cambridge University
    Press, 1968.
    These essays explain a closely argued hypothesis about the
    evolution of Jane Austen's mature novels from her early work;
    they also include a very good assessment of her usually under-
    rated Letters.
PHILLIPS, K. C. *Jane Austen's English*, André Deutsch, 1970.

Essays and monographs on individual novels:

Sense and Sensibility
TANNER, TONY.   Preface to Penguin edition, 1969.
WATT, IAN.   'On *Sense and Sensibility*', in Watt's collection above.

Pride and Prejudice
BRADBROOK, F. W.   Preface to the Oxford English Novels edition, 1970.
BROWER, R. A.   'Light and bright and sparkling: irony and fiction in *Pride and Prejudice*', in his *Fields of Light*, Oxford University Press, New York, 1962.
RUBINSTEIN, E., ed.   *Twentieth-century Interpretations of 'Pride and Prejudice'*, Spectrum Books, 1969.

Mansfield Park
TRILLING, LIONEL.   '*Mansfield Park*', in his *The Opposing Self*, Secker & Warburg, 1955; a modified version appears in *The Pelican Guide to English Literature: From Blake to Byron*, Penguin, 1957.
TANNER, TONY.   Preface to Penguin edition, 1966.
FLEISHMAN, AVROM.   *A Reading of 'Mansfield Park'*, University of Minnesota Press, 1967.

Emma
KETTLE, ARNOLD.   '*Emma*', in his *Introduction to the English Novel*, vol. 1, Hutchinson, 1967; also in Watt's collection above.
LODGE, D.   *Jane Austen's 'Emma': a Selection of Critical Essays*, Macmillan (Casebook series), 1968; Papermac, 1968.
BOOTH, WAYNE C. 'Control of Distance in Jane Austen's *Emma*' in his *The Rhetoric of Fiction*, University of Chicago Press, 1961.
BURROWS, J. F.   *Jane Austen's 'Emma'*, Sydney University Press, London, Methuen, 1969.

Northanger Abbey
MCKILLOP, A. D.   'Critical realism in *Northanger Abbey*', in Watt's collection above.

Persuasion
WRIGHT, A. H.   '*Persuasion*', in Watt's collection above.

Short Biographies

Jane Austen's family

AUSTEN, CASSANDRA, 1739–1827. Jane Austen's mother. A member of the family of Leigh of Adlestrop, Gloucestershire. Her grandfather was brother-in-law to the Duke of Chandos, whose mansion of Canons is probably satirized by Pope as Timon's Villa *(Moral Essays: Epistle to Burlington)*. Her uncle was a famous Master of Balliol and her father a Fellow of All Souls. Among her ancestors, one sheltered Charles I in 1642; hence perhaps Jane Austen's early Stuart sympathies. She married George Austen at Walcot Church, Bath, in 1760.

AUSTEN, CASSANDRA, 1773–1845. Jane's only sister, and fifth child of the family. In her twenties she became engaged to the Reverend Thomas Fowle, who died (before they could marry) in the West Indies, where he was an army chaplain. She lived with her mother till the latter's death, and then continued alone at Chawton. Spent much time with her other relatives, especially her favourite brother, Edward, at Godmersham in Kent. The majority of Jane Austen's letters were written to her, and she seems to have been responsible for destroying many.

AUSTEN, CHARLES JOHN, 1779–1852. Youngest son of the family. Some of the lighter Juvenilia were written for his entertainment. He entered the navy and became an admiral. Married twice, in 1807 and 1820, and had seven children in all.

AUSTEN, EDWARD, 1768–1852. Third son. Adopted when a boy by his father's relative, Thomas Knight of Godmersham, Kent; became his heir and took his name. Married in 1791 and had eleven children, the eldest of whom, Fanny, was Jane Austen's favourite niece. Knighted in 1812. He settled his mother and sisters in 1809 in a cottage on his Hampshire estate at Chawton.

AUSTEN, FRANCIS WILLIAM, 1774–1865. Sixth child and fifth son of the family. Naval officer; he became an admiral and was knighted in 1837. Married twice, in 1806 and 1828, and had seven children by his first wife. He believed that Captain Harville in *Persuasion* was partly founded on himself.

AUSTEN, GEORGE, 1731–1805. Jane Austen's father. Son of a Tonbridge surgeon. Educated at an uncle's expense at Tonbridge and St John's, Oxford, where he became a Fellow. Married in 1760; took orders and obtained the livings of Steventon (1761) and Deane (a mile away) in 1773. Retired to Bath in 1801. Eight children, of whom Jane was the second youngest.

AUSTEN, GEORGE, 1766–1838. Second son. Scarcely anything is known about him, but it is clear that his mental and physical health made it necessary for him to live apart from his family.

AUSTEN, HENRY THOMAS, 1771–1850. Fourth son; Jane's favourite brother. Educated at home and St John's, Oxford. Became Captain and Adjutant of the Oxford Militia. In 1797, he married his cousin, Eliza de Feuillide, and was for many years a prosperous London banker, but went bankrupt in 1815. In 1817 he took orders and became curate at Bentley, near Alton, Hampshire. He wrote the first *Biographical Notice* of his sister prefixed to the first edition of *Northanger Abbey and Persuasion* (1818). Married a second time in 1820.

AUSTEN, JAMES, 1765–1819. Eldest of the family. Educated at home and St John's, Oxford, where he edited a periodical, *The Loiterer*. Took orders and became curate at Deane, succeeding his father as rector of Steventon in 1800. Married twice—in 1792 and 1797. By his second wife he had a son, James Edward Austen, later Austen-Leigh, who wrote the first full-length biography of his aunt: the *Memoir* of 1870.

HANCOCK, ELIZABETH, 1761–1813. Daughter of Jane Austen's mother's sister, who married a surgeon in Bengal. Warren Hastings was Elizabeth's godfather. In 1781 she married Jean Capotte, Comte de Feuillide, and visited Steventon several times. She seems to have been the chief stimulus to the family theatricals there. Her husband was guillotined in 1794, and in 1797 she married Jane's brother Henry. She is sometimes considered to have been the model for Mary Crawford in *Mansfield Park*.

BRYDGES, SIR SAMUEL EGERTON, 1762-1837. Poet, novelist, bibliographer, genealogist, editor. A distant connection of the Austens, he was also the brother of Jane Austen's most intimate friend, Mrs Anna Lefroy. He was the only literary figure in her circle, and edited Collin's *Peerage of England* which she seems to have studied.

Other names

BURNEY, FRANCES (Madame D'Arblay), 1752–1840. Usually known as Fanny Burney. Daughter of a celebrated music scholar. Novels: *Evelina* (1778); *Cecilia* (1782); *Camilla* (1796); *The Wanderer* (1814). A lady in waiting to Queen Charlotte from 1787 to 1791. Married General D'Arblay, a refugee from the French Revolution, in 1793. Her literary fame chiefly depends on her first novel and on her diaries and letters.

COWPER, WILLIAM, 1731–1800. A member of a long-established land-owning family more recently prominent in the law, he himself failed in the profession owing to a mental breakdown, and lived for the rest of his life in retirement. He first joined the household of Morley Unwin, a country rector at Huntingdon, and then continued with his widow, Mary, at Olney, Buckinghamshire. He came under the influence of a prominent evangelical, John Newton, with whom he collaborated in producing the Olney Hymns (1773). He then took to secular verse, especially under the influence of Lady Austen; he published a volume in 1782 and his most famous poem, *The Task* in 1785. He is also famous for the charm of his letters.

DEFOE, DANIEL, 1660–1731. Of Puritan stock, he began his career as a merchant in London, but quickly made a reputation as a political journalist, at first chiefly on the Puritan side, but later working some-times for the Tories, sometimes for the Whigs. Towards the end of his life, his employers found him politically too unreliable, and from retirement he produced his succession of tales which were almost un-precedented in their graphic realism: *Robinson Crusoe* (1719); *A Journal of the Plague Year* (1722); *Moll Flanders* (1722); *Roxana* (1724). These four are the most famous.

FIELDING, HENRY, 1707–54. He began his career as a playwright and manager of the London Haymarket Theatre. He turned to fiction in 1741, when he wrote a burlesque of Richardson's *Pamela* (1740). This preceded *Joseph Andrews* (1742), a more serious attempt to parody Richardson. In 1743 he wrote the satirical novel *Jonathan Wild*, and his masterpiece, *Tom Jones*, was published in 1749. His last novel, *Amelia* (1752), was written when his health was declining. Fielding also had a distinguished career as Chief Magistrate for London and Middlesex.

JOHNSON, SAMUEL, 1709–84. The son of a learned Lichfield book-seller, he was dogged by poverty during his youth and young man-hood. After leaving Oxford without a degree, he eventually came to London to earn his living by writing. He worked for *The Gentleman's Magazine* as a political reporter and published two satirical poems, which began to make his name, *London* (1738) and *The Vanity of Human Wishes* (1749). He edited and largely wrote his own periodical, *The Rambler* (1750–52). He wrote and published *Rasselas* in 1759, by which time his famous Dictionary had also been published. By the 1760s he was regarded as the most important man of letters of the age. His prestige was largely based on his moral and literary criticism.

GILPIN, WILLIAM, 1724–1804. A Hampshire clergyman whose wide reputation was based on his guidebooks to picturesque scenery in the United Kingdom and his *Essay on Prints* (1768) for amateurs of art.

HASTINGS, WARREN, 1732–1818. An officer of the East India Company, appointed Governor General of Bengal in 1773. His activities in support of British interests led to his prosecution for malpractice on his return, but he was acquitted of the charges in 1795. His son was put in the care of Jane Austen's parents while still an infant, but he died at the age of six. He was the godfather of Jane Austen's cousin, Elizabeth Hancock (q.v.).

REPTON, HUMPHRY, 1752–1818. The most distinguished landscape gardener ('improver') in Jane Austen's lifetime. He took to this work on the death of his famous predecessor, Lancelot Brown, in 1782. He was sometimes satirized, notably as Marmaduke Milestone in Peacock's novel *Headlong Hall* (1816).

RICHARDSON, SAMUEL, 1689–1761. A London printer who took to writing novels in consequence of his deep interest in the art of letter-writing. *Pamela, or Virtue Rewarded* (1740) made him immediately famous, but his masterpiece is his second novel, *Clarissa* (1747–8). His third and last novel, *Sir Charles Grandison* (1753) was a less successful attempt to create an ideal hero in emulation of his two ideal heroines. All three novels are in the epistolary form, which Richardson invented.

SCOTT, SIR WALTER, 1771–1832. An Edinburgh lawyer with strong antiquarian interests, he first made a reputation as a poet (*The Lay of the Last Minstrel,* 1805; *Marmion,* 1808; *The Lady of the Lake,* 1810;) and published his first novel, *Waverley,* in 1814. This was followed by *Guy Mannering* (1815), *The Antiquary* (1816), *Rob Roy* (1817), and *The Heart of Midlothian* (1818). He was one of the chief founders of the *Quarterly Review* in 1809, in which he published his laudatory review of *Emma* in 1816.

SHAFTESBURY, ANTHONY ASHLEY COOPER, 3rd EARL OF, 1671–1713. Grandson of the first earl, who had been Charles II's leading opponent. He was keenly interested in politics, but his health was poor, and he gave himself up to moral philosophy. His essays published under the title of *Characteristics of Men, Manners, Opinions, Times* (1711) expressed an optimistic philosophy which had a wide influence in France and Germany as well as Britain.

SHERIDAN, RICHARD BRINSLEY, 1751–1816. The best playwright in Jane Austen's lifetime. His most famous plays are *The Rivals* (1775), *The School for Scandal* (1777) and *The Critic* (1779). After this he took to politics, and was one of the chief prosecutors of Warren Hastings (qv). Some of his plays were among those performed by the Austens in their home-made theatre.

Jane Austen's Vocabulary

Jane Austen's use of words seldom presents major difficulty to readers, but changes in the meaning and emphasis of some words are worth noting. The subject is treated at length by K. C. Phillips in his book *Jane Austen's English,* to which this section is much indebted.

apparent   now: what seems the case. In JA sometimes: what is evidently the case.

ascertain   now: to find out. In JA: to make certain.

candour   now: frankness, bluntness. In JA nearly always: warm sympathy, freedom from malice.

character   now: qualities that identify any individual. In JA often: public image, repute.

canvass   (v) now: to seek support, eg in political votes. In JA: to discuss.

collect   now: to bring together separate objects, form a group. In JA: (often) to infer, deduce.

comfortable   now: feeling easy and contented, especially in body. In JA it sometimes has the older and stronger meaning of 'fortifying to the mind'.

complacency   now: self-satisfaction. In JA: satisfaction (without the disparaging connotation, except when she speaks of 'self-complacency.')

countenance   now: often synonymous with 'face'. In JA usually: the expression on the face.

development   now: (of character) change, growth. In JA: self-revelation over a period of time.

discontent   now: (often) blameworthy dissatisfaction. In JA the word is usually without this unfavourable implication.

discover   now: to find out. In JA: expose, reveal.

disgusting   in JA the word had a milder meaning than it has today, and was used similarly to our word 'distasteful'.

elegance   now: refined and tasteful, usually in outward appearance. In JA: rather more what we mean by 'distinguished', and used about the mind or character as well as the appearance.

expensive   now: costing a lot of money. In JA: extravagant in spending.

experimental now: testing, by putting into practice, especially in scientific contexts. In JA: known by experience.

evil in JA often used mildly, to express 'disagreeable consequence'.

genius now: person or personal quality with rare and original capacity. In JA: often used to express a less exceptional talent or distinction.

genteel now: usually used sarcastically to express artificial refinement. In JA: refined, without sarcastic implication.

horrid now: disagreeable, unpleasant, often in a humorous context. In JA: adjective of 'horror', used much as we use 'horror' in the phrase 'a horror film'.

improve in JA often used in a semi-technical context to mean 'enhance the appearance (of an estate or garden) by the art of landscaping'.

indulge in JA the word lacks its modern unfavourable implications and meant simply 'to allow oneself to take pleasure in'.

irritable now: in a state of annoyance, bad temper. In JA: upset, in slight agitation.

lounge (v) now: to loll about. In JA: to stroll, saunter.

mind now: often synonymous with 'brain' or 'intellect'. In JA: the word implies the essential inner qualities or the self, not exclusively or necessarily the intellectual ones.

nice now: usually, 'pleasant', 'agreeable'. In JA: usually 'exact' or 'precise'.

notice (v) now: observe, give brief attention to. In JA: often 'to treat with special attention'.

oppress now: tyrannize, treat with cruelty. In JA: overwhelm, give excessive attention to (a person).

particular now: detailed, special, not general. In JA: embarrassingly unusual, odd.

peculiar now: often as JA uses 'particular'. In JA: often as we use 'particular'.

person in JA often used to express the sense of 'external appearance'.

precise now: exact, meticulously careful. In JA: fussy, over-conscientious.

prevent now: to stop from happening. In JA: to act or happen in advance of something else happening.

quality   in JA sometimes used as a collective noun for 'the smart people', 'fashionable circle'.

quiz   now: seldom used. In JA: as a noun, 'an amusing oddity', 'absurdity'. As a verb, 'to tease'. 'to make fun of'.

rational   now: in accordance with reason. In JA: acceptable to a reasonable mind.

repulsive   now: very disgusting. In JA: generally, 'unforthcoming', 'cold in manner'.

respectable   now: often 'stuffily conformist'. In JA: usually, 'deserving respect'.

sensible   now: reasonable, rational. In JA: often, 'conscious', 'aware'.

sly   now: cunning in an underhand way. In JA: indirect in manner, not necessarily with implications of deceitfulness.

stout   now: inclined to fatness. In JA: in good health; firm in opinion.

superior   in JA, the word was quite without the ironic overtones of such a modern phrase as 'superior people'.

tease   now: to make fun of, usually playfully. In JA: to vex, annoy.

tolerable   now: endurable. In JA: acceptable, as good as to be expected.

understanding   in JA used much as we use 'mind' (qv); the rational faculty, intelligence.

Places

Much of the information given here is derived from four guidebooks published by Spottiswoode Ballantyne:

AUSTEN-LEIGH, EMMA. *Jane Austen and Steventon*, 1937; *Jane Austen and Bath*, 1939.

AUSTEN-LEIGH, EMMA, and AUSTEN-LEIGH, R. A. *Jane Austen and Lyme Regis*, 1946.

AUSTEN-LEIGH, R. A. *Jane Austen and Southampton*, 1949.

Steventon, Hampshire

The village where Jane Austen was born and where she spent the first twenty-five years of her life. The old rectory (see illustration on page 148) was pulled down in 1828. The church still stands, with a monument to her on the north side of the nave. Her brother James, who succeeded their father in the incumbency, is buried with his second wife in the churchyard, and there are monuments to him and to his first wife Anna in the chancel. The manor house, leased in the Austens' times to the Digweed family, still stands. The neighbouring village of Deane was held in conjunction with the living of Steventon by Jane Austen's father, and the parsonage was inhabited by James Austen before he succeeded his father as rector of Steventon in 1800.

The village of Ashe is two miles from Deane. The former rectory was inhabited by Isaac Lefroy, whose wife was Jane Austen's best friend. Anne Lefroy's death by a fall from her horse in 1804 was commemorated by Jane Austen's one surviving serious poem (included in the *Minor Works*, Oxford edition, vol. VI) written five years later.

Other houses in the neighbourhood and mentioned in the Letters are Ashe Park, Oakley Hall, and Manydown Park where the Austen girls stayed when they were attending balls at Basingstoke (nearly nine miles from Steventon). It was inhabited by a family called Bigg-Wither, whose daughters were also close friends of Cassandra and Jane.

Bath

Two relatives of Jane Austen's mother had residences in Bath: James Leigh Perrot, her mother's brother, rented a house there (No. 1, The Paragon), and her mother's widowed sister retired there. Jane Austen may have visited either several times, but visits are only recorded in 1797 and 1799. In 1801, after Mr Austen's retirement, the Austen family lived in Bath at 4, Sydney Place for at least three years: a plaque on the house commemorates the fact. After Mr Austen's death, they continued in the city some months longer—at 27 Green Park Buildings and at 25 Gay Street.

It was in 1799 that occurred the strange case of the arrest of Mrs Leigh Perrot on a charge of thieving from a shop in Bath: two sets of lace were found in her shopping basket instead of the one that she had bought. If she had been found guilty she would have been executed or transported, but the evidence indicated that her accusers were disreputable and had probably hoped to gain money by blackmail. The case has been described by Sir Frank D. MacKinnon in his book *Grand Larceny, being the Trial of Jane Leigh Perrot, Aunt of Jane Austen.*

Bath is the scene of nineteen chapters of *Northanger Abbey*, and nine of *Persuasion*. Most of the settings in the six novels are fictional, and of the four that are real (the others are London in *Sense and Sensibility*, Portsmouth in *Mansfield Park*, and Lyme Regis in *Persuasion*) only Bath is conveyed with any topographical extensiveness and distinctiveness of character. At least a score of streets and buildings, nearly all (the only important exception is the White Hart Inn) still standing, are mentioned in the two last published novels. Some crucial scenes occur in the Lower Assembly Rooms (Catherine's meeting with Mr Tilney), the Pump Room (her meeting with Isabella Thorpe, see illustration on page 111), the theatre (her apology to Mr Tilney), the Upper Assembly Rooms (the concert in *Persuasion*), and the White Hart Inn, on the site of which the Pump Room Hotel now stands. It is possible to identify the house rented by the Elliots in Camden Place (now Camden Crescent) since 'their house was undoubtedly the best' in the terrace, and must surely be the one surmounted by a pediment bearing the Camden arms. It is possible to trace the course of the reconciliatory walk taken by Captain Wentworth and Anne Elliot from Milsom Street back to her father's house in Camden Place at the end of the novel.

Jane Austen's parents were married at Walcot Church, near the Paragon where her uncle had a house, and her father lies buried in its crypt.

Southampton

After leaving Bath, the Austen family moved to Southampton and lived in Castle Square for about three years; the house has been pulled down.

Lyme Regis

Jane Austen visited Lyme in 1804. The 300-yard ancient jetty known as The Cobb is still in existence (see illustration on page 130); it was in jumping from the higher level to the lower level of this that Louisa Musgrove had her nearly fatal accident. Number 29 Marine Parade has been suggested as Captain Harville's house. A house called 'Wings' has been traditionally regarded as the one Jane Austen inhabited during her 1804 visit, and bears a plaque saying so.

Chawton

In 1809, Jane Austen's brother Edward, who had been adopted by Thomas Knight of Godmersham Hall, Kent (see illustration on page 8) offered his mother and sisters a small house near his own Chawton Manor, not far from Steventon. They accepted it, and it was from here that the six novels emanated in their final form (see frontispiece). It is now the Jane Austen Museum. She lived there until the year of her death, when she moved to lodgings in Winchester to be nearer her doctor. Chawton village is on the outskirts of Alton, on the road to Winchester.

Winchester

In 1817 Jane Austen moved to lodgings in College Street, Winchester (see illustration on page 160) where she was under the treatment of Mr Giles King Lyford, surgeon in ordinary at the county hospital. The house belonged to a Mrs David, and bears a plaque commemorating her death there. Jane Austen is buried in Winchester Cathedral.

Kent

Jane Austen visited her brother Edward at Godmersham in Kent (see page 8), and between 1794 and 1813 took the opportunity of writing parts of her novels there. It has been claimed that Chevening Place that she saw during these visits provided the original for the Rosings estate of *Pride and Prejudice*. On this question readers should consult the book in which this has been argued and documented: David Waldron Smithers, *Jane Austen in Kent* (Hurtwood Publications, 1981).

Harlestone Park, Northants. This house is said to be the original for the mansion of Mansfield Park.

Notes to Maps of Places in Jane Austen's Novels

Northanger Abbey

Catherine Morland's home is the parsonage of the fictional village of Fullerton in Wiltshire, where the story begins and ends. From there she moves to Bath—evidently an easy journey—and from Bath by an equally easy journey to the imaginary house Northanger Abbey, in Gloucestershire.

Northanger Abbey is a medieval house converted to the taste of an eighteenth-century landed proprietor, just as General Tilney is something like a rapacious medieval baron who operates on the principles of a 'polite' eighteenth-century heiress-hunter.

Sense and Sensibility

At the opening of the novel, Elinor and Marianne Dashwood are living with their mother in their family home, Norland Park, a country house in some unspecified part of Sussex. From there they move to Barton Cottage on the estate of Barton Park, a 'large and handsome' house belonging to Sir John Middleton. It is also imaginary, but supposed to be situated near Exeter. Barton Park is evidently the expression of substantial wealth and comfort without much evidence of taste or grandeur. Much of the narrative is also set in London.

Pride and Prejudice

The Bennet family live on a modest estate at the imaginary village of Longbourn in Hertfordshire, near the imaginary country town of Meryton. These have been identified with Ware and Hertford, or with Hemel Hempstead and Watford, respectively. Mr Darcy's mansion of Pemberley in Derbyshire is situated five miles from the imaginary town of Lambton. It is a grand house 'standing well on rising ground, and backed by a ridge of high woody hills'; Elizabeth 'had never seen a place for which nature had done more, or where natural beauty had been so little counteracted by an awkward taste'. It is clearly intended to represent a high standard in which taste and style harmonize with nature and function. The mansion of Lady Catherine de Burgh, Rosings, is situated near the real town of Westerham in West Kent. It represents ostentation rather than genuine distinction of taste and style. Some scenes also occur in London.

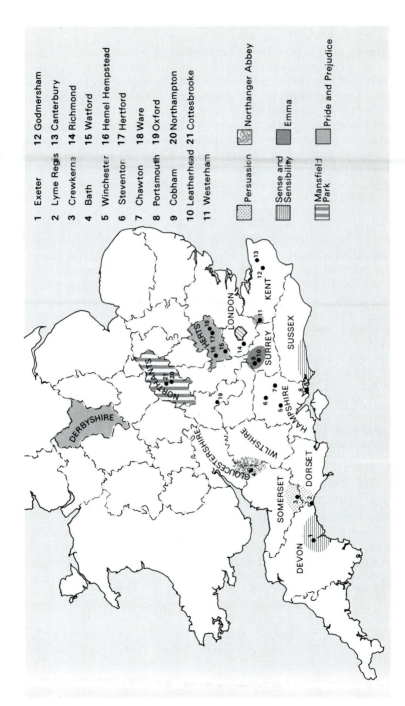

1 Exeter
2 Lyme Regis
3 Crewkerne
4 Bath
5 Winchester
6 Steventon
7 Chawton
8 Portsmouth
9 Cobham
10 Leatherhead
11 Westerham

12 Godmersham
13 Canterbury
14 Richmond
15 Watford
16 Hemel Hempstead
17 Hertford
18 Ware
19 Oxford
20 Northampton
21 Cottesbrooke

Northanger Abbey

Persuasion

Emma

Sense and Sensibility

Mansfield Park

Pride and Prejudice

Mansfield Park

Mansfield Park is situated near Northampton, and may correspond to the neighbourhood of Cottesbrooke. It represents the unimaginative but substantial and rational taste embodied in its proprietor, Sir Thomas Bertram. Mr Rushworth's Sotherton Court is an Elizabethan mansion and represents a tradition which has been entirely lost, at least by its owner. Rushworth wishes to 'improve' it elaborately and expensively, without reference either to the rational standards represented by Mansfield Park or to the historical rootedness of the Elizabethan character of the house itself. The house of Mansfield Park is thought to be based on Harlestone Park, in Northamptonshire.

Emma

The novel is situated in the imaginary town of Highbury in Surrey, supposed to be 16 miles from London, 9 from Richmond, and 7 from Box Hill. Leatherhead and Cobham have both been suggested as possible foundations for it. Emma's home, Hartfield, is supposed to be based on Polesden Lacey, a modest and gracious eighteenth-century house in southern England. Mr Knightley's house, Donwell Abbey, is grander and older, surrounded by a much larger estate—'its ample gardens stretching down to meadows washed by a stream, of which the Abbey, with all the old neglect of prospect, had scarcely a sight—and its abundance of timber in rows and avenues, which neither fashion nor extravagance had rooted up'. Mr Knightley represents the best style of traditional landlord, who balanced the good sense cultivated in his own period by the traditional sense of community with his tenants.

Persuasion

The novel begins at Sir Walter Elliot's mansion of Kellynch Hall, near the imaginary village of Uppercross, in the neighbourhood of the actual town of Crewkerne, south-western Somerset. It is expensively run, and suggests the ostentation which the pompous Sir Walter thought appropriate to his rank. The Great House, belonging to the Musgroves of Uppercross, is unpretentious, but the Musgroves, like their houses, were in a state of alteration. The father and mother were in the old English style, and the young people in the new. Most of the narrative takes place in Bath and Lyme Regis.

Notes to Maps of London and Bath

The interest of these maps is that they show with what precision Jane Austen placed her characters in the appropriate social background.

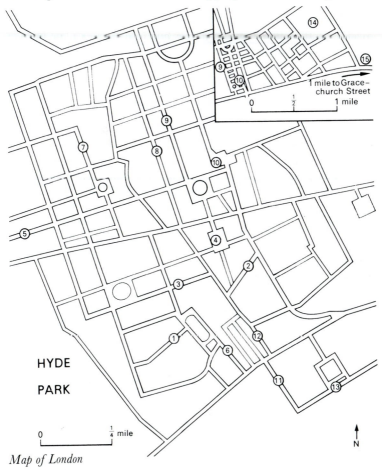

1 mile to Grace-
church Street

Map of London

London

The smart, rich areas were Mayfair and the newer streets and squares between Oxford Street and Regent's Park. Bond Street, then as now, was the most fashionable shopping street; the great men's clubs were shortly to begin to be built in Pall Mall. To take the novels in their order.

Sense and Sensibility
Sir John Middleton (2) has a house in Conduit Street, east of Bond Street; his sister-in-law, Mrs Palmer (4), is in Hanover Square, and her mother, Mrs Jennings (6), in Berkeley Street, off Portman Square. The John Dashwoods (9) inhabit Harley Street, and Colonel Brandon (11) St James's Street. The bachelors, Willoughby (12) and Edmund Ferrars (13) have rooms in Bond Street and Pall Mall respectively. All these are rich, or have rich connections, and they live within walking distance of one another. The poor and vulgar Steeles on the other hand (15) live much farther east, in Bartlett Buildings, off Holborn Circus.

Pride and Prejudice
Mr Hurst (3), Bingley's rich brother-in-law, lives in Grosvenor Street, but Elizabeth Bennet's homespun uncle and aunt, Mr and Mrs Gardiner, live in Gracechurch Street in the City. Elizabeth Bennet remarks satirically that Mr Darcy might be able to travel so far, but that he would find the air very contaminating.

Emma
Mr and Mrs Churchill (7) take a house in Manchester Street, half way between Oxford Street and Regent's Park, although later they establish themselves at Richmond, for the sake of the purer air. The John Knightleys (14) on the other hand, live in Brunswick Square, Holborn. This square was newly built and elegant though not in a smart district, but it is characteristic of John Knightley's 'no-nonsense' attitude to society that he would prefer to live away from the smart districts and closer to his professional business.

Mansfield Park
The rich and worldly Admiral Crawford (1) lives at possibly the smartest address of all—Hill Street, off Berkeley Square, and the rich Mrs Rushworth (8) lives in Wimpole Street.

Bath

The old town was enclosed in the bend of the river Avon. When the city became fashionable in the eighteenth century, the smart streets were built to the north of this, up the hill to the height (by about 1790) of 400 feet. Another fashionable area, built in the last twenty years of the century, grew up east of the river, constituting the so-called 'new town'.

Northanger Abbey
General Tilney (1) has rooms in Milsom Street. This street was the heart of the fashionable district, corresponding rather to Bond Street in London. The Allens and Catherine Morland (6) stay in Pulteney Street in the new town. The Thorpes (8) are at Edgar Buildings, Queen Square. They are social adventurers, vulgarians on the make. Queen Square was one of the earliest streets in the reconstruction of

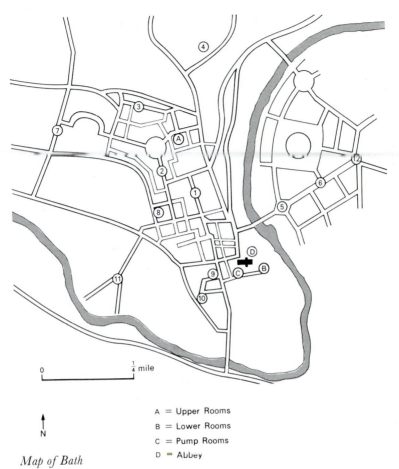

A = Upper Rooms
B = Lower Rooms
C = Pump Rooms
D = Abbey

Map of Bath

Bath, and had declined in fashionability. The Musgrove girls (in *Persuasion*) refuse it scornfully.

Persuasion

Most of the well-to-do characters live up the hill from Queen Square: Admiral Croft (2) in Gay Street, Captain Wallis (7) in Marlborough Buildings, Lady Russell (3) in Rivers Street, and the Elliots (4) highest of all, in Camden Place. But the socially most exalted, the Dowager and Lady Dalrymple (5) live in the new town, Laura Place. The Musgroves (9) stay in the town's principal inn, the White Hart. At the other extreme, the impoverished Mrs Smith (10) lives down in the heart of the old town, near Westgate Buildings.

The Austens themselves (11 and 12) lived at one time not far from Mrs Smith, in Green Park Buildings, but they also lived at a rather better address at the far end of the new town, in Sidney Terrace

Index